RENEWED PRIMARY FRAMEWORK

100 MATHS HOMEWORK ACTIVITIES

YEAR 3

Ann Montague-S...
and Richard Coo...

9.2009

0
510.
7
ONE

◻ Credits

Authors
Ann Montague-Smith
Richard Cooper

Development Editor
Nicola Morgan

Editor
Sara Wiegand

Assistant Editor
Margaret Eaton

Illustrations
Garry Davies (Beehive Illustration)
Mark Ruffle (Beehive Illustration)

Series Designer
Helen Taylor

Designer
Macmillan Publishing Solutions

UNIVERSITY OF CHICHESTER

Mixed Sources
Product group from well-managed
forests and other controlled sources
www.fsc.org Cert no. TT-COC-002769
© 1996 Forest Stewardship Council

Text © Ann Montague-Smith and
Richard Cooper
© 2009 Scholastic Ltd

Designed using Adobe InDesign

Published by Scholastic Ltd
Villiers House
Clarendon Avenue
Leamington Spa
Warwickshire CV32 5PR

www.scholastic.co.uk

Printed by Bell and Bain Ltd, Glasgow

1 2 3 4 5 6 7 8 9   9 0 1 2 3 4 5 6 7 8

British Library Cataloguing-in-Publication Data
A catalogue record for this book is available from the British Library.

ISBN 978-1407-10218-4

The rights of Ann Montague-Smith and Richard Cooper to be identified as
the authors of this work have been asserted by them in accordance with the
Copyright, Designs and Patents Act 1988.

Extracts from the Primary National Strategy's *Primary Framework for
Mathematics* (2006) www.standards.dfes.gov.uk/primaryframework © Crown
copyright. Reproduced under the terms of the Click Use Licence.

Contents

Homework

Homework: Counting, partitioning and calculating

Homework: Securing number facts, understanding shape

Homework: Handling data and measures

Homework: Calculating, measuring and understanding shape

Homework: Securing number facts, relationships and calculating

Puzzles and problems

Answers

About the series

100 Maths Homework Activities offers a complete solution to your planning and resourcing for maths homework activities. There are six books in the series, one for each year group from Year 1 to Year 6.

Each *100 Maths Homework Activities* book contains 72 homework activities, which cover the Renewed Framework objectives, and 36 puzzles and problems, which focus on the Using and applying objectives.

About the homework activities

Each homework activity is presented as a photocopiable page, with some supporting notes for parents and carers provided underneath the activity. Teachers' notes relating to the activities appear in grid format at the beginning of each block's activities. When exactly the homework is set and followed up is left to your professional judgement.

Across the *100 Maths Homework Activities* series, the homework activities cover a range of homework types. Some of the activities are for sharing. These encourage the child to discuss the homework task with a parent or carer, and may, for example, involve the home context, or a game to be played with the carer. Other activities involve investigations or problem-solving tasks. Again, the parent or carer is encouraged to participate in the activity, offering support to the child, and discussing the activity and its outcomes with the child.

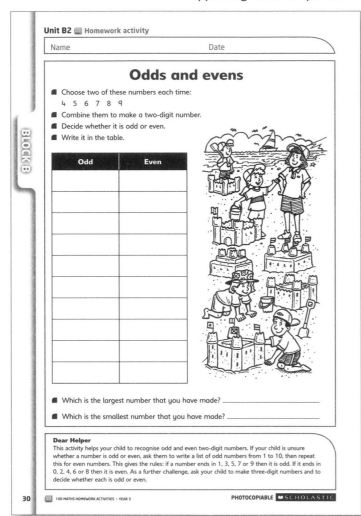

Using the homework activities

Each homework page includes a 'Helper note', which explains the aim of the homework and how the adult can support their child if he or she cannot get started. It is recommended that some form of homework diary be used alongside these activities, through which to establish an effective home–school dialogue about the children's enjoyment and understanding of the homework. A homework diary page is provided on page 6 of this book.

Teachers' notes

The teachers' notes appear in a grid format at the start of each block's homework activities. Each grid contains the following information:

- the Framework unit
- the homework activity's title
- a brief description of the format and content of the activity, which will help you to decide which homework activity to choose
- the Renewed Framework learning objective/s
- a 'Managing the homework' section which provides two types of help – 'before' and 'after'. The 'before' notes provide suggestions for ways to introduce and explain the homework before the children take it home. These notes might include a brief oral activity to undertake as preparation for the homework. The 'after' notes provide suggestions for how to manage the review of the homework when the children return with it to school. Suggestions include discussing strategies used for solving a problem, comparing solutions, and playing a game as a class.

About the puzzles and problems

The puzzles and problems (pages 90-107) provide coverage of the Using and applying mathematics objectives and can be used very flexibly to provide children with a comprehensive range of fun maths tasks to take home. The grid displayed on page 89 shows which puzzles and problems cover each of the Using and applying objectives.

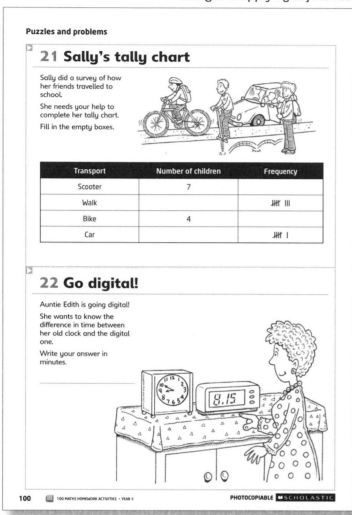

Puzzles and problems

21 Sally's tally chart

Sally did a survey of how her friends travelled to school.

She needs your help to complete her tally chart.

Fill in the empty boxes.

Transport	Number of children	Frequency
Scooter	7	
Walk		JHT III
Bike	4	
Car		JHT I

22 Go digital!

Auntie Edith is going digital!

She wants to know the difference in time between her old clock and the digital one.

Write your answer in minutes.

100   100 MATHS HOMEWORK ACTIVITIES · YEAR 3   PHOTOCOPIABLE ■SCHOLASTIC

The puzzles and problems are based on work that the children will be covering during the year and should test their skills at that level. Some of the questions may be solved quickly, others will require more thought. Either way, children should be encouraged to try a variety of different approaches to solving problems and to look for clues and patterns in maths. It is essential for them to read the question carefully (sometimes more than once) to understand exactly what they are being asked to do. A few of the puzzles and problems will require an everyday household item or the help of a family member. Most should be readily solved by a child working on their own.

Remind the children that if a problem or puzzle is proving too difficult or frustrating, they could leave it and come back to it later with a refreshed mind!

Developing a homework policy

The homework activities have been written with the DCSF 'Homework guidelines' in mind. These can be located in detail on the Standards website **www.standards.dfes.gov. uk/homework/goodpractice** The guidelines are a good starting point for planning an effective homework policy. Effective home-school partnerships are also vital in ensuring a successful homework policy.

Encouraging home-school links

An effective working partnership between teachers and parents and carers makes a positive impact upon children's attainment in mathematics. The homework activities in this book are part of that partnership. Parents and carers are given guidance on what the homework is about, and on how to be involved with the activity. There are suggestions for helping the children who are struggling with a particular concept, such as ways of counting on or back mentally, and extension ideas for children who would benefit from slightly more advanced work.

The homework that is set across the curriculum areas for Year 3 should amount to a total of about one and a half hours per week. The homework diary page, which can be sent home with the homework activity with opportunities for a response from the parents/carers, can be found on page 6 of this book.

Using the activities with *100 Maths Framework Lessons Year 3*

The activities covered in this book fit the planning within the book *100 Maths Framework Lessons Year 3* (also published by Scholastic Ltd). As teachers plan their work on a week-by-week basis, so the homework activities can be chosen to fit the appropriate unit of work.

Homework diary

Name of activity & date sent home	Child's comments		Helper's comments	Teacher's comments
	Did you like this activity? Draw a face. ☺ 😐 ☹ a lot / a little / not much	How much did you learn? Draw a face. ☺ 😐 ☹ a lot / a little / not much		

Counting, partitioning and calculating

Activity name	Learning objectives	Managing the homework
A1		
Number match Match numerals and number words for HTU numbers.	Read, write and order whole numbers to at least 1000	**Before:** Explain that the homework will help the children to read and write numbers using figures and words. **After:** Review the homework together. Discuss particularly the numbers 203 and 230, and what the 2, 0 and 3 represent in each of the numbers.
Partitioning Partition three-digit numbers into H, T and U.	Partition three-digit numbers into multiples of 100, 10 and 1 in different ways	**Before:** Write 456 on the board and ask what each digit represents. **After:** Mark the homework together. Check that the children understand what each digit represents. Note how long they took to complete the homework.
Counting patterns Write counting sequences in steps of three, four and five.	Count on from and back to zero in single-digit steps	**Before:** Count in threes, fours and fives from and back to zero, then from any small number. **After:** Invite the children to suggest their own counting patterns in threes, fours and fives, from and back to any small number.
Number order Order given numbers onto a number line.	Read, write and order whole numbers to at least 1000	**Before:** Draw an empty number line on the board and write some three-digit numbers. Ask the children to add these to the line in order. **After:** Review the homework together, discussing any issues that arise.
A2		
Addition Review addition strategies by choosing a strategy to solve each addition question.	Add or subtract mentally combinations of one-digit and two-digit numbers	**Before:** Explain that you would like the children to identify which of the three strategies they should use to solve each question. Remind them of what the strategies are. **After:** Mark the homework as a class and invite suggestions as to which strategy should be used for each question, and why that is the best one to choose.
Times 10 and 100 Timed exercise of multiplying single-digit and two-digit numbers by 10, then by 100.	Multiply one-digit and two-digit numbers by 10 or 100, and describe the effect	**Before:** Ask: *What happens to the digits when we multiply by 10... by 100?* **After:** Review the homework together, encouraging the children to say the division sentences, such as 500 ÷ 100 and 500 ÷ 10.
Race track challenge Choose sets of four small numbers to make totals.	Add or subtract mentally combinations of one-digit and two-digit numbers	**Before:** Explain that you would like the children to use the strategy of putting the largest number first when tackling this homework. **After:** Review together which numbers the children combined and how they totalled them. Discuss which methods were most efficient.
Add these Decide whether to use mental methods or pencil and paper to complete some additions.	Add or subtract mentally combinations of one-digit and two-digit numbers	**Before:** Review the mental strategies that the children have learned for addition. Remind them that sometimes they will find it helpful to use pencil and paper too. **After:** Review the homework together. Discuss which strategies the children chose (and why) for each question.

Counting, partitioning and calculating

Activity name	Learning objectives	Managing the homework
A3		
Find the difference Timed exercise for finding small differences by counting up.	Add or subtract mentally combinations of one-digit and two-digit numbers	**Before:** Remind the children of the strategy of counting up from the smaller number to the larger to find small differences. **After:** Mark the work together. Invite children from each ability group to demonstrate how they found the answers.
Adding and adjusting Choose from a selection of near multiples of 10 to add to a set of two-digit numbers.	Add or subtract mentally combinations of one-digit and two-digit numbers	**Before:** Read through the homework instructions with the children and check that they understand what they have to do. **After:** Ask for answers from the children. If anyone has invented their own puzzle, ask them to share it with the class.
Add and subtract Use empty number lines to add and subtract.	Develop and use written methods to record, support or explain addition and subtraction of two-digit and three-digit numbers	**Before:** Write up some examples of addition and subtraction using an empty number line and work through these together. **After:** Mark the homework together and discuss any difficulties or issues that the children had.
Division problems Solve a range of division problems; decide whether to round up or down to find the solution.	Use practical and informal written methods to support multiplication and division of two-digit numbers (for example, 13 × 3, 30 ÷ 4); round remainders up or down, depending on the context	**Before:** Say: *There are 35 children in the class. Everyone would like a biscuit. If biscuits come in packs of ten, how many packs do I need?* Discuss how the answer will round up to 4. **After:** Review the homework, discussing for each question whether the answer rounds up or down.

SCHOLASTIC

BLOCK A

| Name | Date |

Number match

Draw a line to match the numbers to the number words.

Numbers
56
100
167
203
490
622
999
230
765
899

Number words
One hundred and sixty seven
Four hundred and ninety
Nine hundred and ninety nine
Seven hundred and sixty five
Six hundred and twenty two
Fifty six
Two hundred and thirty
Two hundred and three
Eight hundred and ninety nine
One hundred

- Choose three numbers from the following list:

  1 6 7 0

- Write the number you make using numerals.
- Write it again in words.
- Do this three more times.

Number using numerals	Number in words

Dear Helper

This activity helps your child to read and write numbers with three digits in figures and words. Encourage your child to read through both sets of numbers, and to say both sets out loud before finding matching pairs. If your child finds it difficult to find the matching pairs, encourage them to look at the first digit, say it, then find a number word that is the same. They can then check the second digit and number word in the same way. As an additional challenge to the second part of the sheet, encourage your child to make as many numbers as they can, writing these in figures on the back of this sheet, then writing the same numbers using words.

Name   Date

Partitioning

- Write these three-digit numbers as hundreds, tens and units. The first one is done for you.
- See how quickly you can do this!
- Draw hands on the first clock face to show when you start.
- Draw hands on the second clock face to show when you finish.
- I took ☐ minutes to do this.

Number	Hundreds	Tens	Units
167	100	60	7
649			
333			
509			
590			
950			
905			
237			

- Write four three-digit numbers of your own in the first column of this grid.
- Now write them in hundreds, tens and units.

Number	Hundreds	Tens	Units

Dear Helper
This activity helps your child to partition, or separate, three-digit numbers into hundreds, tens and units. If your child is confident with this, they should manage the first part of the activity very quickly. If your child is unsure, ask them to write the number again, under the headings H, T and U. Now ask how much each of the digits is worth. For example, in 123, the 1 is worth 100, the 2 is worth 20 and the 3 is worth 3. If your child would like a further challenge, ask them to choose four digits and write as many three-digit numbers as they can, using just these digits.

Name	Date

Counting patterns

◼ Write a number pattern for counting in 3s.
- ☐ Decide which number from 0 to 2 you will start on.
- ☐ Continue the pattern until the boxes are all full.

◼ Now write a counting pattern for counting in 4s.
- ☐ Decide which number from 0 to 3 you will start on.
- ☐ Continue the pattern until the boxes are all full.

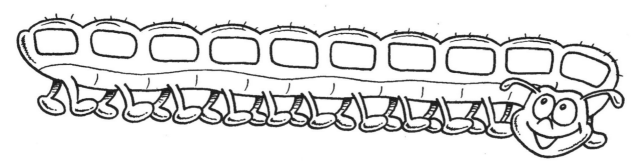

◼ Write a counting pattern for counting in 5s.
- ☐ Decide which number from 0 to 4 you will start on.
- ☐ Continue the pattern until the boxes are all full.

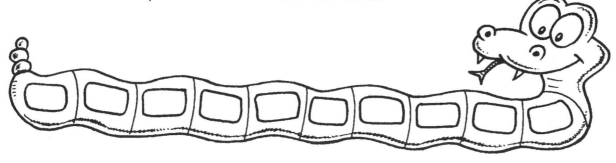

Dear Helper
This activity helps your child to count on from a small number in threes, fours and fives. If your child is unsure, ask them to write out the numbers from 0 to 30. Now say: *Which number shall we start on for counting in threes?* Then circle each number that comes in the pattern. Challenge your child to write patterns for counting in sixes, starting on any number from 0 to 5.

BLOCK A

Name   Date

Number order

■ Write these sets of numbers in order, starting with the smallest, on the empty number lines.

■ See how quickly you can do this.

165 156 651 615 516 561

831 901 879 910 887 897

501 516 499 504 497 500

■ Now choose three of these digits and make a three-digit number: 4 8 5 9

■ Write the number in the boxes below.

■ Do this three more times on the back of the sheet. Write the numbers in order, starting with the smallest.

Dear Helper

This activity helps your child to order three-digit numbers. If your child is unsure of how to begin, ask them to look at the hundreds digits first. They can then find the lowest of these, or maybe two that are the same. Now ask them to look at the tens digits and find the lowest of these, and finally the units digits. This will help them to order the numbers, smallest to largest. Challenge your child to choose any three digits, make as many three-digit numbers as they can from these, and position them, in order, on a number line.

Name   Date

Addition

- Read each of these addition questions carefully.
- Decide how you will tackle the problem. You could:
  - ☐ Put the larger number first and count on.
  - ☐ Find near doubles using doubles that you already know.
  - ☐ Bridge through a multiple of 10 then adjust.
- Write your answer.
- Now put a tick in the column to show which strategy you used.

Question	Answer	Counting on	Using doubles	Bridging
45 + 10				
78 + 6				
34 + 35				
49 + 30				
60 + 28				
84 + 9				
26 + 25				
27 + 70				
41 + 42				
94 + 7				

- Explain to someone at home how you worked out the answer to each of these.

Dear Helper
This activity gives your child the opportunity to use addition strategies. For example, putting the larger number first and counting on: 7 + 24 = 24 + 7 = 31; using near doubles: 34 + 35 could be seen, for example, as double 30 add 4 add 5; bridging through multiples of 10: this could be used for 45 + 30, which is 45 + 10 + 10 + 10 = 75. If your child finds any of these strategies difficult to use, or is unsure about which strategy to use, then work through the question together, identify the best strategy and write out the steps on paper. If your child enjoys a challenge, then ask them to write their own questions on the back of this sheet, one for each strategy.

Name	Date

Times 10 and 100

◀ In the grid below, multiply the first number by 10.

☐ Now multiply it by 100.

☐ Do the same for the other numbers.

☐ See how quickly you can do this!

◀ Draw hands on the first clock face to show when you start.

◀ Draw hands on the second clock face to show when you finish.

Start number	×10	×100
5		
8		
4		
9		
7		
1		
10		
30		
80		
90		

Start

Finish

◀ Now write three more of these multiplications, choosing your own numbers.

Start number	×10	×100

◀ I took [   ] minutes to do this homework.

Dear Helper

This activity helps your child to understand what happens when we multiply by 10 and by 100. If your child is unsure, write a number such as 2 and say: *What is 2 times 10?* Write the 20 underneath, lining up the 2 of '2' with the '0' of the 20. Now repeat this for multiplying 2 by 100, again lining up the tens and units digits. Encourage your child to explain how the digits shift one place to the left for ×10, and two places for ×100. Challenge your child to divide their answers by 100 and by 10 to check.

Name	Date

Race track challenge

- Each car on the race track has a number.
- Choose four of the car numbers.
- Write the numbers in the order in which you will total them. Remember to put the largest number first.
- Write the totals.

Dear Helper
This activity encourages your child to add several small numbers, beginning with the largest number. Once your child has chosen their set of numbers, discuss where they will start, and in which order they will total the other numbers. If they find this difficult, remind them of other strategies to try. For example, for 14 + 5 + 4 + 6 they could look for a pair that makes 10 (4 + 6) so 14 + 10 + 5 = 24 + 5 = 29. To take it further, challenge your child to try totalling more than four small numbers.

BLOCK A

Name   Date

Add these

- Write the answers to these addition sentences.
- Decide whether to use mental methods or a paper-and-pencil method such as an empty number line.
- Tick the box for the strategy that you used.

Question	Answer	Tick the strategy you used	
		Mental methods	Paper and pencil
9 + 5 + 6 + 4			
6 + 8 + 4 + 7			
5 + 9 + 8 + 4			
17 + 4 + 8 + 3			
15 + 8 + 5 + 9			
13 + 5 + 7 + 8			
12 + 14 + 6 + 5			
19 + 13 + 7 + 2			
16 + 5 + 12 + 8			
19 + 7 + 4 + 6			

- Now find three different ways to make a total of 30. Use four numbers each time.

☐ + ☐ + ☐ + ☐ = ☐

☐ + ☐ + ☐ + ☐ = ☐

☐ + ☐ + ☐ + ☐ = ☐

Dear Helper

This activity helps your child to use mental strategies such as: putting the largest number first; finding two numbers that make a 10; adding numbers such as 9, 11 and 19 by adding 10 or 20 and adjusting by 1. If your child is unsure about the mental strategies, they may find it helpful to use a paper-and-pencil method, such as partitioning the numbers (for example, 8 + 9 + 7 = 9 + 1 + 7 + 7 = 10 + 14 = 24). Alternatively, they may find it helpful to use an empty number line. Encourage your child to explain which method they would prefer to use for each question. If they still find this difficult, discuss which method might be good to try, and talk this through together. As an additional challenge, encourage your child to write four further number sentences, this time to make a total of 50.

Name	Date

Find the difference

🔲 Write the difference between each pair of numbers.

 🔲 Remember: to do this you can count up from the smaller number to the larger.

 🔲 See how quickly you can do this!

🔲 Draw hands on the first clock face to show when you start.

🔲 Draw hands on the second clock face to show when you finish.

First number	Second number	Difference
16	19	
18	24	
38	42	
87	93	
45	51	
62	57	
52	47	
45	52	
96	87	
98	102	

Start

Finish

🔲 I took ☐ minutes to do this.

Dear Helper

This activity helps your child to practise counting up from the smaller to the larger number in order to find a small difference. If they find this difficult, they may find it helpful to use an empty number line. Ask your child to label one end with the smaller number, then to decide how many to count on, in ones if necessary, to reach the larger number. Now suggest they look for steps on the way. For example, for 34 – 29 they could say *29 and 1 is 30, and 4 more is 34. 1 + 4 is 5, so the difference between 34 and 29 is 5*. You could extend the activity by challenging your child to try some questions with larger numbers, such as finding the difference between 197 and 205.

Name   Date

Adding and adjusting

- Choose a number from the first grid.
- Add 19, 21, 29 or 31 to it.
- See if you can find your answer in the second grid. If it is there, put a cross through it.
- Repeat this until all the numbers in the second grid have been crossed out.

45	65	56	57	52
34	69	28	29	62

75	58	64	49	73
86	86	63	100	81

Dear Helper
This activity helps your child to use the strategy of adding the closest multiple of 10 and adjusting by 1.
So, for 45 + 19 this would be 45 + 20 – 1. If your child is unsure about how to begin, suggest that
they start with the first number (45), adding on 19, 21, and so on until they find the answer in the
second grid. Discuss their addition strategy, and, if this will help, suggest that your child writes out the
number sentence of 45 + 19 = 45 + 20 – 1 until they are confident with using this strategy. As a further
challenge, ask your child to make up a similar puzzle to try with their friends back at school.

Name　　　　　　　　　　　　　　　　　Date

Add and subtract

🔲 Use the empty number lines to help you to find the answers to these addition and subtraction sentences.

45 + 36 = ☐

65 – 28 = ☐

84 + 68 = ☐

84 – 67 = ☐

93 + 78 = ☐

91 – 56 = ☐

121 + 59 = ☐

123 – 35 = ☐

145 + 92 = ☐

342 – 97 = ☐

Dear Helper

This activity encourages your child to use an informal pencil-and-paper method, before they are introduced to more formal methods in the next school year. If your child is unsure about how to start, for the addition, ask them to write the larger number onto the empty number line, then to count up in tens and then units until they reach the answer. They should mark the steps on the line, as shown *right*. For subtraction, ask your child to write the number to be taken away onto the number line, then to count up to the second number like this: To calculate 65 – 28: start at 28: 28 and 2 to 30; 30 and 30 to 60; and 5 more to 65.

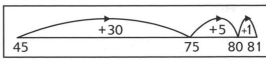

So 65 – 28 = 2 + 30 + 5 = 37. Challenge your child to do these questions as quickly and accurately as they can.

Name   Date

Division problems

■ Write the answers to these questions.

    □ Remember to think about whether you
need to round up or down to find the answers.

    □ There is room to make jottings.

There are 34 children in Class 3. Each child needs a new jotter. Jotters come in packs of ten. How many packs are needed? ☐	The children in Class 3 have been invited to a party. They will travel there in cars. Each car will hold four passengers. How many cars are needed? ☐
The children in Class 3 have been invited to the cinema. Tickets come in books of six at £5 a book. How many ticket books are needed? ☐ How much will this cost? ☐	The school buys apples to sell at playtime. The apples are put out in baskets, with ten apples in each basket. There are 54 apples. How many baskets can be filled? ☐

Dear Helper
This activity helps your child to use multiplication facts to find division facts, and to decide whether to round the answer up or down, depending on the question. Ask your child to read the question with you, and decide whether the answer will round up or down. If your child is unsure about this, talk about the division and whether there is a remainder and how to deal with this for this question. Challenge your child to complete the questions as quickly and accurately as they can.

BLOCK A

Securing number facts, understanding shape

Activity name	Learning objectives	Managing the homework
B1		
Is it true? Investigate the properties of squares and rectangles to show that a general statement is true.	Identify patterns and relationships involving numbers or shapes, and use these to solve problems	**Before:** Remind the children that a statement about shapes can be true or false and that they need to find examples to demonstrate this. **After:** Review the children's findings. Discuss how the properties of rectangles are the same as squares, but that squares have a unique property (all sides equal in length).
Odd numbers Find examples to match the statement that any odd number plus any even number always gives an odd answer.	Identify patterns and relationships involving numbers or shapes, and use these to solve problems	**Before:** Remind the children that the activity asks them to find examples that match the statement. **After:** Invite children from each ability group to write one of their addition sentences on the board. Discuss how an odd number plus an even number always gives an odd answer.
Find the change Solve money problems involving choosing coins and change.	Represent the information in a puzzle or problem using numbers, images or diagrams; use these to find a solution and present it in context, where appropriate using £.p notation	**Before:** Explain the task to the children and tell them that they may use real coins to help them at home. **After:** Ask individual children to explain how they found their results.
Presents Problems to solve where children decide which operation to use.	Represent the information in a puzzle or problem using numbers, images or diagrams; use these to find a solution and present it in context, where appropriate using £.p notation	**Before:** Remind the children that they can choose the method to solve a problem. **After:** Discuss which mathematics, and way of calculating, the children chose. Discuss which were the more efficient methods, and why.
Check it Addition sentences to be checked with an equivalent calculation.	Use knowledge of number operations and corresponding inverses, including doubling and halving, to estimate and check calculations	**Before:** Write 20 + 25 on the board. Ask how this could be calculated and how to check the answer. **After:** Review the worksheet together, discussing in particular the check calculations chosen.
Making shapes Investigate which new shapes can be made by cutting an original shape.	Identify patterns and relationships involving numbers or shapes, and use these to solve problems	**Before:** Discuss the homework task together. Explain that the children should cut off the pieces from the sheet, then sketch each result on another sheet of paper. **After:** Review together the range of shapes that the children found and how they did this. Ask them to suggest extensions to the problem.
B2		
Money puzzle Find different totals of three coins.	Represent the information in a puzzle or problem using numbers, images or diagrams; use these to find a solution and present it in context, where appropriate using £.p notation	**Before:** Explain the activity and suggest that some children may find it helpful to use real coins to help them to solve the puzzle. **After:** Review the homework and write the totals on the board. Ask: *What would be the largest possible total?* (£6) *How did you work that out? What is the smallest possible total?* (60p)
Odds and evens Make two-digit numbers and decide whether each is odd or even.	Identify patterns and relationships involving numbers or shapes, and use these to solve problems	**Before:** Revise the rules for odd and even numbers. **After:** Invite the children to give some examples of odd and even numbers. Extend this to three-digit examples for the more confident children.
Sticker problems Solve some word problems set in a real-life context.	Solve one-step and two-step problems involving numbers, money or measures, including time, choosing and carrying out appropriate calculations	**Before:** Explain to the children that they will need to use their answer to one question to solve the next, and so on. **After:** Review the homework together. Discuss the strategies that the children used to solve the problems.

Securing number facts, understanding shape

Activity name	Learning objectives	Managing the homework
Equivalent fractions Identify equivalent fractions in a range of shapes.	Read and write proper fractions (for example, $3/7$, $9/10$), interpreting the denominator as the parts of a whole and the numerator as the number of parts; identify and estimate fractions of shapes; use diagrams to compare fractions and establish equivalents	**Before:** Explain that the children are to write two fractions (such as ½ and $2/4$) that are equivalent to the shaded part of each shape. **After:** Invite the children to discuss which fractions they shaded. Discuss the range of possible answers.
Fraction match Play a fraction pelmanism game.	Read and write proper fractions (for example, $3/7$, $9/10$), interpreting the denominator as the parts of a whole and the numerator as the number of parts; identify and estimate fractions of shapes; use diagrams to compare fractions and establish equivalents	**Before:** Remind the children of some equivalent fractions. Write ½ on the board and ask for suggestions of equivalent fractions. **After:** The children can play the game in pairs for a few minutes as a starter activity.
Is it symmetrical? Identify lines of symmetry, and shapes with no symmetry.	Draw and complete shapes with reflective symmetry and draw the reflection of a shape in a mirror line along one side	**Before:** Remind the children that not all shapes have lines of symmetry, and that some shapes have more than one line of symmetry. **After:** Mark the homework together, checking that the children are clear about where the lines of symmetry are.
B3		
Sorting 2D shapes Recognise the properties of 2D shapes.	Relate 2D shapes and 3D solids to drawings of them; describe, visualise, classify, draw and make the shapes	**Before:** Check that the children know what a quadrilateral is and can suggest some examples. **After:** Review the work together. Ask the children to suggest other properties for each of the shapes.
Calculation check Solve a number sentence and write a check calculation.	Use knowledge of number operations and corresponding inverses, including doubling and halving, to estimate and check calculations	**Before:** Explain to the children that for each number sentence they are expected to write a check calculation. **After:** Review the homework, paying particular attention to the check calculations. Discuss whether these were sensible ones, and why the children think that.
Measures word problems Solve word problems set in the context of measures, deciding which way to calculate.	Solve one-step and two-step problems involving numbers, money or measures, including time, choosing and carrying out appropriate calculations	**Before:** Remind the children that they can use mental methods, mental methods with jottings, and pencil-and-paper methods to solve these problems. **After:** For each problem, discuss the chosen methods and why these were chosen to solve the problem.
What's my shape? Find shapes to satisfy a general statement.	Relate 2D shapes and 3D solids to drawings of them; describe, visualise, classify, draw and make the shapes	**Before:** Say: *I am thinking of a 2D shape with no straight sides. What could my shape be?* Discuss the possibilities. **After:** Review the homework together. Discuss the children's findings and how they worked out their answers.
Where does it fit? Compare fractions and order them onto a number line.	Read and write proper fractions (for example, $3/7$, $9/10$), interpreting the denominator as the parts of a whole and the numerator as the number of parts; identify and estimate fractions of shapes; use diagrams to compare fractions and establish equivalents	**Before:** Draw a number line labelled from 0 to 1 and ask the children to place fractions such as ½ and ¾ onto it. **After:** Mark the homework together and check that the children can order fractions on a number line with reasonable accuracy.
Fraction measure Estimate fractions of measurements.	Read and write proper fractions (for example, $3/7$, $9/10$), interpreting the denominator as the parts of a whole and the numerator as the number of parts	**Before:** Remind the children that measures can be seen as fractions of the whole unit (for example, nearly 50cm is about ½ a metre). **After:** Review the homework together. Ask the children which questions they found most difficult and why. Discuss the answers so that all understand.

Name	Date

Is it true?

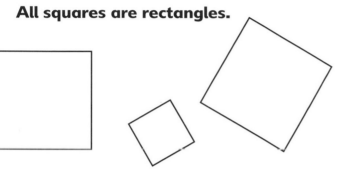

◼ Investigate this sentence:

All squares are rectangles.

◼ Think about the properties of a rectangle. Write them in the box below.

◼ Now write a sentence to explain if the statement '**All squares are rectangles**' is true.

_____

_____

_____

Dear Helper

This activity helps your child to think about general statements about shape. All squares are rectangles, because rectangles have four right angles and opposite sides that are equal in length. This applies to squares, but squares are special because all of their sides are the same length. If your child is unsure, look at the drawings of the squares, then draw some rectangles and discuss their similarities. You could challenge your child to explain why all squares are quadrilaterals, but all quadrilaterals are not squares.

BLOCK B

Name	Date

Odd numbers

◼ Read this sentence:

Any odd number can be made by adding an odd number and an even number.

◼ Write some addition sentences to show that this is true.

Dear Helper
This activity helps your child to think about general statements about numbers. If your child is unsure how to begin, suggest that they choose two small numbers (one odd and one even), then write an addition sentence like this: 5 + 6 = 11, then another one such as 41 + 40 = 81. Ask: *Is the answer odd or even?* Now encourage your child to write some more of these addition sentences to show that the statement is true. Challenge your child to consider whether an odd number plus an odd number always gives an even total.

Name	Date

Find the change

■ Marcus bought a pencil. The pencil cost 16p. He paid for it with one coin.

■ Find four different ways Marcus could have paid.

■ Write as a subtraction sentence to find the change each time.

Marcus chose a ☐ coin.

☐ p – ☐ p = ☐ p

So his change was ☐ p.

Marcus chose a ☐ coin.

☐ p – ☐ p = ☐ p

So his change was ☐ p.

Marcus chose a ☐ coin.

☐ p – ☐ p = ☐ p

So his change was ☐ p.

Marcus chose a ☐ coin.

☐ p – ☐ p = ☐ p

So his change was ☐ p.

BLOCK B

Dear Helper

This activity helps your child to calculate the change due from various coins. If your child is unsure, ask: *Which coin could Marcus use?* Encourage your child to realise that any coin worth less than 20p would not be enough. You may wish to provide some coins to help your child to calculate the change. To extend the activity, challenge your child to provide the change from £2 for other amounts less than £2.

Name   Date

Presents

◗ Yasmin wants to buy a present for everyone in her family. She has £10 to spend. She lives with her mother, father and brother Ouni. Ouni is eight years old.

◗ Help Yasmin decide what to buy.

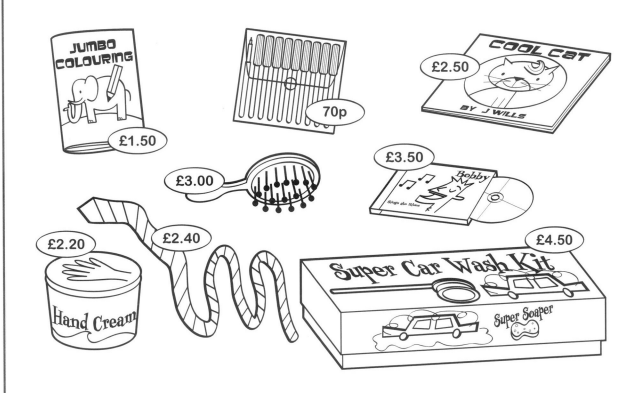

◗ Yasmin bought her mother a _____ . It cost [   ] .

◗ She bought her father a _____ . It cost [   ] .

◗ She bought her brother a _____ . It cost [   ] .

◗ The presents cost [   ] altogether.

◗ Her change from £10 was [   ] .

Dear Helper
This activity helps your child to solve problems, choosing which mathematics to use and how to calculate. Encourage your child to decide which items to buy and to explain how they worked out the total and the change. If your child finds this difficult, they will benefit from using coins to help them to total the amounts and find the change. Challenge your child to work out how much it would cost if Yasmin had bought everything. Ask: *Would £20 be enough?*

Name   Date

Check it

- Write your answers to the number sentences in the answer box.
- Write your check calculation in the checking box.
  - ☐ See how quickly you can do this!
- Draw hands on the first clock face to show when you start.
- Draw hands on the second clock face to show when you finish.

Start

Finish

Number sentence	Answer	Check calculation
40 + 24		
36 + 40		
11 + 7 + 19		
16 + 5 + 8		
19 + 8 + 3		
50 + 37		
20 + 77		
12 + 18 + 6		
31 + 10 + 8		
47 + 40		

Dear Helper
This activity helps your child to find a way of checking their calculations. Your child could, for example, add the numbers in a different order, or they could use subtraction (for example, for 20 + 25 they could try 45 – 20). If your child is unsure, discuss which strategy they might like to try. Your child can use an empty number line if they find this helpful. Challenge your child to complete the work as quickly and accurately as they can.

Name	Date

Making shapes

- ◢ You will need a pair of scissors, a pencil and another sheet of paper.
- ◢ On this sheet there are several L shapes. Cut these out carefully.
- ◢ Now take one of your shapes.
  - ☐ Cut one of the squares and remove a right-angled triangle.
  - ☐ Make as many different shapes as you can by cutting off one right-angled triangle each time. You can only make **one** straight cut each time.
  - ☐ Check each time that you have made a new shape by turning it and flipping it.
  - ☐ Sketch each shape that you make on your other sheet of paper.

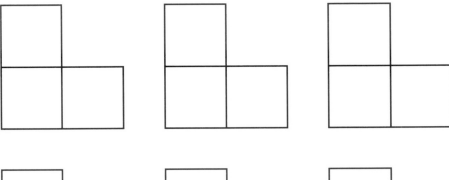

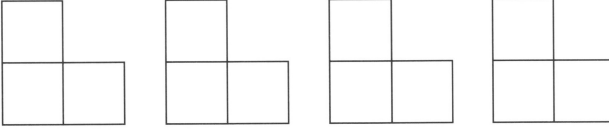

- ◢ How many different shapes did you find?

  _____

- ◢ Now try again. Cut off **two** right-angled triangles each time.

- ◢ How many different shapes can you make now?

  _____

PHOTOCOPIABLE ▮▮SCHOLASTIC

BLOCK B

Name	Date

Money puzzle

◼ Imagine you have three coins. Each coin is worth more than 10p. You can have more than one of the same coin.

◼ Write ten different totals that you can make with different combinations of three coins in the space below.

_____ + _____ + _____ = _____

_____ + _____ + _____ = _____

_____ + _____ + _____ = _____

_____ + _____ + _____ = _____

_____ + _____ + _____ = _____

_____ + _____ + _____ = _____

_____ + _____ + _____ = _____

_____ + _____ + _____ = _____

_____ + _____ + _____ = _____

_____ + _____ + _____ = _____

Dear Helper
This activity helps your child to total money. It is also an investigation. If your child is unsure about how to start, ask: *Which coins could you use?* (20p, 50p, £1 and £2 – the selection could contain a combination of different coins, and some coins could be used more than once in each selection.) Use real coins if this helps and encourage your child to total the coins, starting with the largest coin each time. Challenge your child to order their totals from least to greatest.

Name   Date

Odds and evens

◀ Choose two of these numbers each time:

4   5   6   7   8   9

◀ Combine them to make a two-digit number.

◀ Decide whether it is odd or even.

◀ Write it in the table.

Odd	Even

◀ Which is the largest number that you have made? _____

◀ Which is the smallest number that you have made? _____

Dear Helper

This activity helps your child to recognise odd and even two-digit numbers. If your child is unsure whether a number is odd or even, ask them to write a list of odd numbers from 1 to 10, then repeat this for even numbers. This gives the rules: if a number ends in 1, 3, 5, 7 or 9 then it is odd. If it ends in 0, 2, 4, 6 or 8 then it is even. As a further challenge, ask your child to make three-digit numbers and to decide whether each is odd or even.

BLOCK B

Name	Date

Sticker problems

◾ Jamie likes to collect football stickers. Here are some problems about Jamie and his stickers.

◾ You will need to use the answer to the first problem to solve the next one, and so on.

◾ There is space for you to make jottings.

1. Jamie used his pocket money to buy some stickers. He bought 15 English football stickers, double that number of Scottish stickers, and 20 Welsh ones.

How many stickers did Jamie buy altogether?

2. When Jamie got to school the next day he decided to give his best friend, Jon, half of his Scottish stickers.

How many stickers did Jamie have left in total?

3. On the way home from school Jamie decided to call in to see his cousin, Ellie. Ellie also collects stickers and she has a total of 47 stickers. They looked at their stickers together. Jamie gave Ellie 10 of his stickers.

How many stickers does Jamie have now?

How many stickers does Ellie have now?

4. Jamie's dad gave Jamie another 30 stickers. However, Jamie already had 13 of these so he decided to give the 13 to his friend Jon.

How many stickers does Jamie have now?

Dear Helper

This activity contains lots of detail in each of the problems. If your child is unsure, talk through the problem and agree which information is essential, and which can be ignored. Now work through the problem together, deciding which mathematics is needed to solve it. Challenge your child to invent a further problem about Jamie and his stickers.

Name   Date

Equivalent fractions

- Look carefully at each shape.
- Decide what fraction has been shaded.
- Now write two fractions for the shaded part.
- The first one has been done for you.

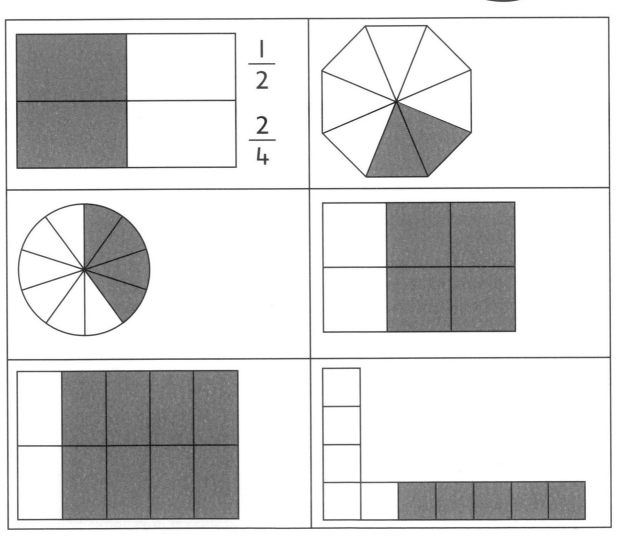

Dear Helper
This activity helps your child to recognise and record two fractions that are equivalent, or worth the same, such as $\frac{1}{2}$ and $\frac{2}{4}$. If your child is unsure about this, encourage them to count how many parts there are in total to the shape and write this as the bottom number of the fraction. Now ask them to count how many parts have been shaded and write this as the top number of the fraction. This gives them one fraction. Discuss how else this could be written – for example, $\frac{6}{10}$ is also $\frac{3}{5}$. You could challenge your child to draw some more shapes, shade equal parts and write two fractions for each. They can do this on the back of this sheet.

BLOCK B

Name	Date

The fraction cards:

$\frac{3}{6}$	$\frac{6}{8}$	$\frac{4}{6}$	$\frac{6}{10}$
$\frac{4}{8}$	$\frac{3}{4}$	$\frac{2}{3}$	$\frac{3}{5}$
$\frac{2}{4}$	$\frac{2}{8}$	$\frac{2}{6}$	$\frac{2}{10}$
$\frac{1}{2}$	$\frac{1}{4}$	$\frac{1}{3}$	$\frac{1}{5}$

Fraction match

■ You can play this game with a partner.

☐ Cut out the fraction cards and shuffle them.

☐ Place the cards face down on the table in front of you.

☐ Now turn over two cards.

☐ If the fractions are worth the same, keep the cards.

☐ If the cards do not match, turn them face down again.

☐ Try to remember where each fraction is!

■ The winner is the player with the most pairs of cards at the end of the game.

Dear Helper

Play this game together. The idea is to make pairs of equivalent fractions, such as $\frac{1}{2}$ and $\frac{2}{4}$, $\frac{1}{3}$ and $\frac{2}{6}$ and so on. If your child is unsure about this, then suggest that they draw the fraction. So, for $\frac{2}{6}$ they could draw a rectangle split into six equal strips and shade in two of the strips. Discuss how this is the same as $\frac{1}{3}$. Challenge your child to play Snap with you using the cards, playing as quickly as possible.

Name	Date

Is it symmetrical?

◼ Look carefully at each shape.

◼ Put a cross through the shapes that have no lines of symmetry.

◼ Draw in the lines of symmetry in the other shapes.

    ◻ Hint: some shapes have one line of symmetry, some shapes have more than one.

    ◻ Use a mirror if you are unsure.

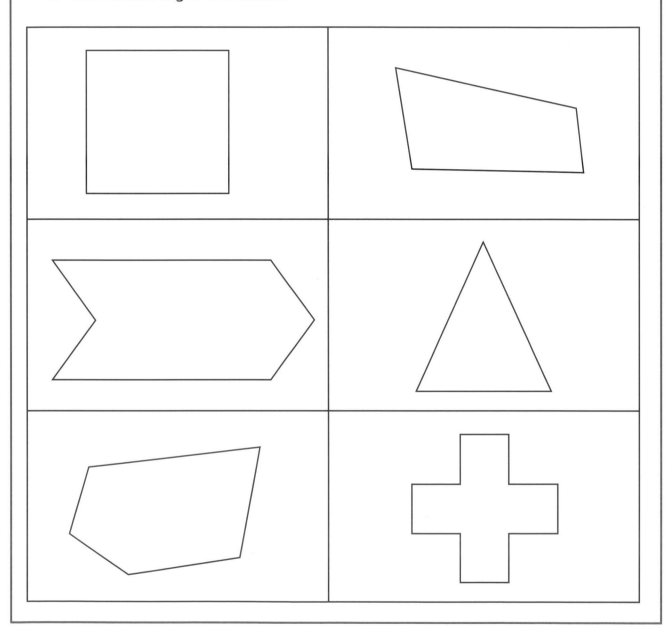

Dear Helper

This activity helps your child to recognise which shapes have lines of symmetry and where the line of symmetry is. If your child finds this difficult, provide a small hand mirror and ask them to place the mirror on one half of the shape, with the mirror standing vertically, so that they can see the shape reflected. By repositioning the mirror, they can check where the lines of symmetry are, and see which shapes have no symmetry. Challenge your child to draw their own symmetrical shapes and to mark in the lines of symmetry.

PHOTOCOPIABLE 📖SCHOLASTIC

Name	Date

Sorting 2D shapes

◼ Look carefully at each shape.

◼ Read each shape description.

◼ Draw a line from each shape to the correct description.

◼ Write the shape's name in the space next to it.

_____

This shape has three sides.
It has a right angle.

_____

This shape is a quadrilateral.
All of its sides are the same length.
All of its angles are the same size.

_____

This shape has no straight sides.
It is symmetrical.

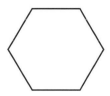

_____

This shape has all of its angles the
same size.
It has no right angles.
It has six sides.

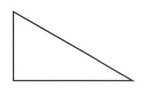

_____

This shape is not a square.
It is a quadrilateral.
It has four right angles.

◼ Sketch some quadrilaterals on the back of this sheet.

◼ Can you sketch three different quadrilaterals?

Dear Helper
This activity helps your child to recognise the properties of some 2D shapes. If your child is unsure about the vocabulary used in the descriptions, read through them together. A quadrilateral is any flat shape with four sides, such as squares and rectangles. To extend the exercise, challenge your child to draw three different pentagons, hexagons and octagons.

Name	Date

BLOCK B

Calculation check

■ Write the answer to each number sentence.

■ Write a check calculation to show that you have the correct answer. Remember, you can check:

☐ subtraction with addition ☐ addition with subtraction ☐ halving with doubling

☐ multiplication with division ☐ division with multiplication

■ See how quickly you can do this. Time how long it takes.

Number sentence	Jottings	Check calculation
26 + 45 =		
42 ÷ 6 =		
92 – 87 =		
16 × 2 =		
Half of 38 =		

■ I took ☐ minutes to do this.

Dear Helper

This activity helps your child to recognise which type of check calculation is appropriate for each operation. If your child is unsure, ask them to explain how they solved the number sentence. Then ask them to think of which operation (+ , –, × or ÷) they could use to take them back to the start number. Challenge your child to find different ways of checking, such as adding in a different order.

Name	Date

Measures word problems

🔲 Decide how to solve each problem.

🔲 Write the answer.

🔲 In the third column of the grid, write how you solved it:

   ☐ **M** for mental calculation

   ☐ **MJ** for mental and jottings

   ☐ **P** for pencil-and-paper method

Problem	Answer	Method
There is 1 litre and 400ml left in the milk bottle. Jan drinks 500ml of the milk. How much is left now?		
A bag of apples weighs 450 grams. A bag of pears weighs twice as much as the apples. How much do the apples and pears weigh in total?		
There are 50 metres of ribbon on the reel. Marcie buys 14 metres of the ribbon and Jane buys $18\frac{1}{2}$ metres. How much ribbon is left on the reel now?		
The film at the cinema starts at 7.30pm. It finishes at 9.45pm. How long does the film last?		

Dear Helper

This activity helps your child to make decisions about how to solve problems. Discuss with your child which way they will solve each problem: mentally, mentally with some jottings, or a paper-and-pencil method such as using an empty number line. Discuss how to record the answer. For the first question, for example, the answer could be recorded in millilitres, as a fraction of a litre or as a decimal fraction of a litre. You could challenge your child to record each answer in at least two different ways.

Name	Date

What's my shape?

- Read the description of each shape.
- Write the name of the shape and sketch a picture of it.

I am a 2D shape. I have four straight sides. I have no right angles. What am I? _____	I am a 3D shape. I have one flat face. I have one curved face. My flat face is circular. What am I? _____
I am a 2D shape. I have one right angle. My three sides are straight. What am I? _____	I am a 3D shape. I have four flat faces which are triangles. I have one flat face which has four sides the same length and all its angles are right angles. What am I? _____
I am a 3D shape. I have one flat face. I have one curved face which meets at a vertex. What am I? _____	I am a 2D shape. I have five equal angles. I have five sides all the same length. What am I? _____

Dear Helper

This activity helps your child to use general statements about shapes. If they find this difficult, read together each line of the description and decide what shapes this could refer to and what shapes do not fit. Challenge your child to write their own general description of a regular shape.

Name	Date

BLOCK B

Where does it fit?

■ Decide where these fractions will fit onto each number line.

1. $\dfrac{1}{2}$ $\dfrac{1}{4}$ $\dfrac{1}{8}$

0 ——————————

2. $\dfrac{1}{3}$ $\dfrac{2}{3}$ $\dfrac{5}{6}$

0 ——————————

3. $\dfrac{1}{4}$ $\dfrac{3}{8}$ $\dfrac{7}{8}$

0 ——————————

■ Now choose three fractions.

■ Write them here.

■ Write the three fractions onto this number line.

0 ——————————

Dear Helper

This activity helps your child to compare and order fractions, placing them in order on a number line. If your child is unsure, compare two of the fractions and ask your child to decide which is larger and which is smaller, and why they think that. They can then compare other pairs in the set in the same way. Challenge your child to choose another set of three fractions and to position these, in order, onto a number line.

Name   Date

Fraction measure

◀ Estimate and write the fraction of each measurement that you can see.

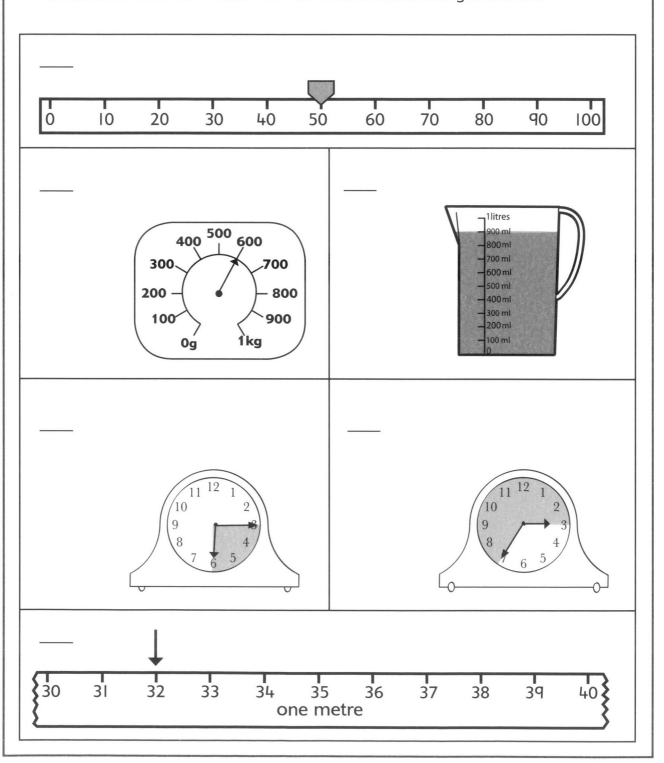

Dear Helper

This activity helps your child to make estimates using fractions. If your child is unsure, discuss what they can see in the picture, and where the reading is. Discuss which the closest reading is, then compare this with the whole. So, for example, the first one reads 50cm, which is ½ of a metre. Challenge your child to complete these estimates quickly and accurately.

Handling data and measures

Activity name	Learning objectives	Managing the homework
C1		
10 centimetres Estimate and measure lengths of 10cm; devise a way of measuring longer items.	Read, to the nearest division and half-division, scales that are numbered or partially numbered; use the information to measure and draw to a suitable degree of accuracy	**Before:** Remind the children how to use a ruler, where to place the item against the ruler, and how to read ½cm. **After:** Review the homework. Discuss how the children used the ruler to measure longer lengths.
Number sort Sort numbers in different ways onto a Carroll diagram.	Use Carroll diagrams to sort data and objects using more than one criterion	**Before:** Remind the children of the key features of a Carroll diagram, ie 'Has' and 'Does not have'. **After:** Invite the children to explain one of their sortings. Discuss the range of sortings they could have chosen.
Measuring up Read and consider facts about measurements and decide if they are correct.	● Know the relationships between kilometres and metres, metres and centimetres ● Choose and use appropriate units to estimate, measure and record measurements	**Before:** Discuss the relationship between the different units of measurement, and the use of the appropriate units to estimate and record. **After:** Review the worksheet together. Invite the children to explain which measurements they thought were correct, and why.
Bird spotting Read the information in a frequency table and use it to answer questions.	Answer a question by collecting, organising and interpreting data; use frequency tables to represent results and illustrate observations	**Before:** Remind the children how to read and understand the information in a frequency table. **After:** Mark the homework together. Discuss how the children used the information in the table to find the answers.
C2		
How heavy? Read scales and write the results for mass.	● Know the relationship between kilograms and grams; choose and use appropriate units to estimate, measure and record measurements ● Read, to the nearest division and half-division, scales that are numbered or partially numbered	**Before:** Practise with the children reading some scales for mass. **After:** Invite children from each group to feed back their answers for the others to check their homework.
Venn diagram sort Sort data onto a one-region Venn diagram.	Use Venn diagrams to sort data and objects using more than one criterion	**Before:** Discuss with the children how to fill in a Venn diagram. **After:** Mark the homework together. Discuss which numbers belong inside the circle and which outside, and why.
Bar charts Interpret data in a bar chart with intervals labelled in twos.	Answer a question by collecting, organising and interpreting data; use bar charts to represent results and illustrate observations	**Before:** Ask the children to look carefully at the bar chart on the homework sheet and to say what its scale is. **After:** Mark the homework together, asking children from each ability group to give answers.
A day at the office Answer questions on time using an analogue clock.	Read the time to the nearest five minutes on an analogue clock; calculate time intervals and find start or end times for a given time interval	**Before:** Read through the activity sheet together to make sure that the children understand the task. **After:** Invite the children to share their answers with the rest of the class.

Handling data and measures

Activity name	Learning objectives	Managing the homework
C3		
Measuring bonanza Choose suitable units for measuring capacities.	Know the relationship between litres and millilitres; choose and use appropriate units to estimate, measure and record measurements	**Before:** Review the relationship between millilitres and litres. **After:** Discuss the children's choices of units and containers.
How much? Read scales for litres and millilitres.	• Know the relationship between litres and millilitres • Read, to the nearest division and half-division, scales that are numbered or partially numbered	**Before:** Put some liquid into containers with scales and invite the children to read off how much is there. **After:** Mark the homework together and discuss any difficulties that the children found.
Jugs of milk Read and mark scales for litres and millilitres.	Read, to the nearest division and half-division, scales that are numbered or partially numbered; use the information to measure and draw to a suitable degree of accuracy	**Before:** Remind the children how to read scales on containers. **After:** Mark the homework together, asking children from each ability group to give answers.
Which video game? Record data as a pictogram.	Answer a question by organising and interpreting data; use pictograms to represent results and illustrate observations	**Before:** Discuss with the children how to record data as a pictogram. Highlight the relationship between the icon and the number it represents. **After:** Review the homework together. Discuss how the children used the information to complete the pictogram.

Name	Date

10 centimetres

- There is a ruler printed for you on this sheet.
- Find something at home which you estimate to be about 10 centimetres long.
- Now measure it as accurately as you can, to the nearest $\frac{1}{2}$ cm.
- Write your estimate and measurement in the table.
- Do this five more times.

I chose	My estimate	My measurement

- Now find something that you estimate to be about 20 centimetres in length.
- Find a way to measure it using the ruler.
- Write what you did here. _____

_____

_____

_____

_____

BLOCK C

Dear Helper

This activity helps your child to estimate and measure lengths using centimetres and half centimetres. If your child is unsure about how to use the ruler, show them how to line up the item to be measured with the '0' on the ruler, and take a reading. To develop this further, challenge your child to estimate and measure things that are about 30cm long.

Name   Date

Number sort

- 🔖 Use the numbers 1 to 20.
- 🔖 Find a way to sort them in the Carroll diagram.
- 🔖 Write headings for the diagram.
- 🔖 Now write in your numbers.

- 🔖 Now find another way to sort the numbers 1 to 20 in this Carroll diagram.

Dear Helper

This activity helps your child to sort by one criterion in a Carroll diagram. When sorting in a Carroll diagram, one set of numbers has a common property (even numbers, for example); the other set does not have this property and would be labelled 'Not even numbers'. The 'not even' numbers are the odd numbers, but are not labelled like that here. Another way of sorting could be 'Numbers less than 10' and 'Numbers not less than 10'. Discuss different ways of sorting the numbers as there are many ways to do this. Challenge your child to find at least another two ways of sorting the numbers 1 to 20.

PHOTOCOPIABLE 📖SCHOLASTIC

Name	Date

Measuring up

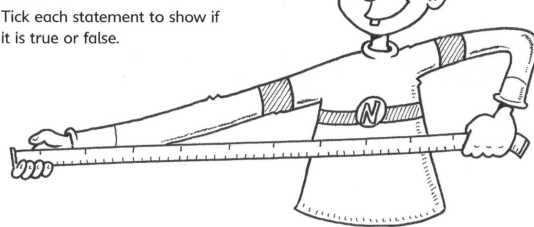

- Read Know-it-all Nigel's facts about measures.
  - ☐ Beware – some of Nigel's information is incorrect!
- Tick each statement to show if it is true or false.

		True	**False**
1.	There are 100cm in a metre.	☐	☐
2.	There are 100m in a kilometre.	☐	☐
3.	My arm is 52m long.	☐	☐
4.	The world record for the high jump is 2.6cm.	☐	☐
5.	I should use a ruler to measure the length of a book.	☐	☐
6.	Half a kilometre is 500m.	☐	☐
7.	Mount Everest is 3500km high.	☐	☐
8.	The distance from London to Brighton is 56m.	☐	☐
9.	I should use a long tape measure to measure the distance of a cricket ball throw.	☐	☐
10.	There are 150cm in one and a half metres.	☐	☐
11.	The moon is roughly 5000cm from the Earth.	☐	☐

Dear Helper
This activity helps your child to understand the relationship between kilometres and metres, and metres and centimetres, and the use of appropriate units of measurement to estimate and record. Give your child an idea of distance so they have a mental picture to help them estimate. For example: a football pitch is roughly 100m long, so a kilometre is roughly the length of ten football pitches; a DVD case is roughly 20cm long, so five DVD cases placed in a line will be roughly a metre.

BLOCK C

Name

Date

Bird spotting

- ◢ Year 3 did a survey over five days.
- ◢ They wrote down the number of wild birds spotted in the playground between 10.30am and 11.00am each morning.
- ◢ This frequency table shows the results of Year 3's survey.
- ◢ Read the information in the table and use it to answer the questions below.

Day	Wild birds spotted
Monday	14
Tuesday	11
Wednesday	0
Thursday	16
Friday	12

1. How many birds were spotted on Tuesday?

_____

2. How many birds were spotted on Thursday and Friday in total?

_____

3. On which day were the most birds spotted?

_____

4. What was the total number of birds spotted over the five days?

_____

5. Give one possible reason why no birds were spotted on Wednesday.

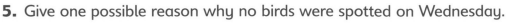

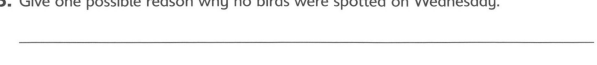

Dear Helper

This activity requires your child to answer questions by reading information from a frequency table. Make sure your child reads the information carefully, and takes time to think about what they are asked to do, before answering the questions. Challenge your child to conduct their own survey at home and draw their own frequency table to show the results.

PHOTOCOPIABLE ◖SCHOLASTIC

Name	Date

How heavy?

- Look carefully at each of these scales.
- Write how much the items on each of the scales weigh.

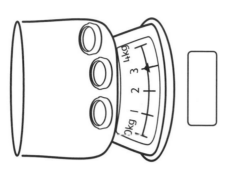

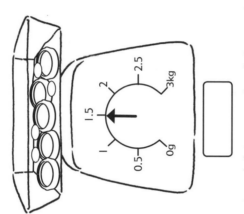

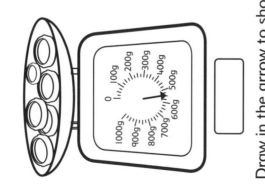

- Draw in the arrow to show the correct weight on each of the scales.

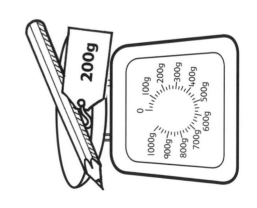

BLOCK C

Dear Helper
This activity helps your child to read from scales and to mark a scale reading accurately. If your child is unsure, ask them to count along the markings on the scale to say what each one represents. For a reading of 400g this will be straightforward, but for 550g your child will need to recognise that this is halfway between the 500g and 600g marks. Challenge your child to suggest where readings such as 750g would come on the scale to 3kg.

Name   Date

Venn diagram sort

- Use the numbers from 20 to 50.
- Sort them in this Venn diagram.

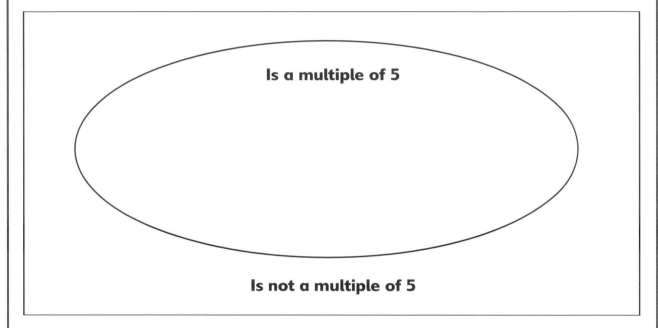

- Now sort the numbers from 20 to 50 in this Venn diagram.

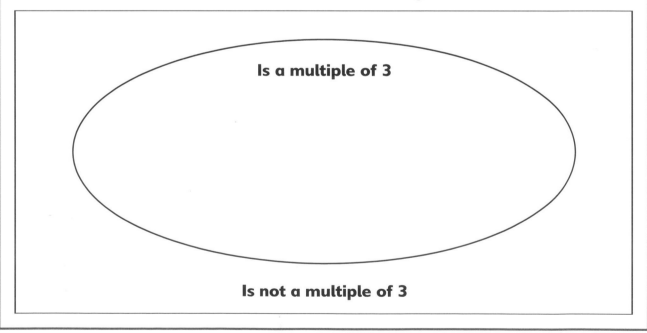

BLOCK C

Dear Helper
This activity helps your child to sort data in a Venn diagram. Inside the top oval your child should put the 'multiple of 5' numbers. Outside the oval, but inside the rectangle, is where all the other numbers should be written. If your child is unsure, suggest that they write out all the numbers from 20 to 50. Now ask them to circle each number that is a multiple of 5. Discuss where these numbers fit in the diagram, and where the other numbers go. Repeat this for multiples of 3/not multiples of 3. Challenge your child to create their own Venn diagram, this time for multiples of 4/not multiples of 4.

Name   Date

Bar charts

■ Use the information in the bar chart to answer the questions below.

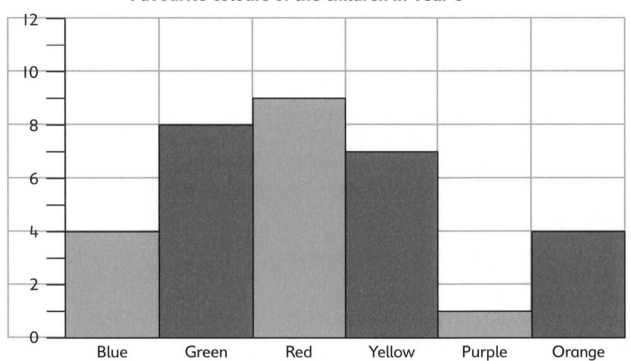

Favourite colours of the children in Year 3

1. How many more children like red than like purple? _____

2. Which is the most popular colour? _____

3. Every child in Year 3 decided on their favourite
   colour. How many children are there in Year 3? _____

4. Which is the least popular colour? _____

5. What is your favourite colour? _____

BLOCK C

Dear Helper
This activity helps your child to interpret data in a bar chart where the intervals are labelled in twos.
This means that every square in this chart represents two children. If your child is unsure about the scale,
count up the green column in twos to see how many there are. Do this for the red column and discuss
how the column ends halfway between 8 and 10 (9). Challenge your child to find some data about their
family and draw a bar chart for this, with a scale of one square representing two things.

Name	Date

A day at the office

◾ Here is what happened on Rob's first day at work. He always needs to be on time!

◾ Draw the hands on a clock face to answer each question.

1. The car journey to work takes Rob 20 minutes.
He needs to be at work at 9 o'clock.
At what time should he leave?

2. Rob had a meeting with his boss which lasted
40 minutes.
It started at 9.30am.
At what time did the meeting end?

3. Lunchtime! Rob's new colleagues took him out
to lunch at 1.00pm.
They came back 50 minutes later.
At what time did they return from lunch?

4. Rob spent $2\frac{1}{2}$ hours working on his computer.
He started at 2.00pm.
At what time did he finish on the computer?

5. At 5.00pm Rob spent 50 minutes in a traffic
jam trying to get home!
At what time did he escape the traffic jam?

6. At 8.10pm Rob watched TV for $1\frac{1}{2}$ hours
before going to bed.
At what time did he go to bed?

Dear Helper
Your child will benefit greatly if they wear a watch when learning to tell the time. A watch can be bought very cheaply. Looking at clocks around the home will also help. Ask your child questions about time and encourage them to read clock faces to tell you the time.

Name	Date

Measuring bonanza

◼ Decide which measurement to use when measuring the capacity of each of these containers. Tick the correct box.

	Measure in litres	Measure in millilitres

◼ Look around you at home. Make two lists on the back of this sheet:
- ☐ Things measured in millilitres
- ☐ Things measured in litres

Dear Helper
This activity helps your child to recognise which units would be best to measure capacity in each situation in the pictures. Discuss each picture with your child and encourage them to come to a decision about which would be best in each case, and to explain why. In addition to the second part, you could challenge your child to write a list of things outside the home that are measured in litres.

Name   Date

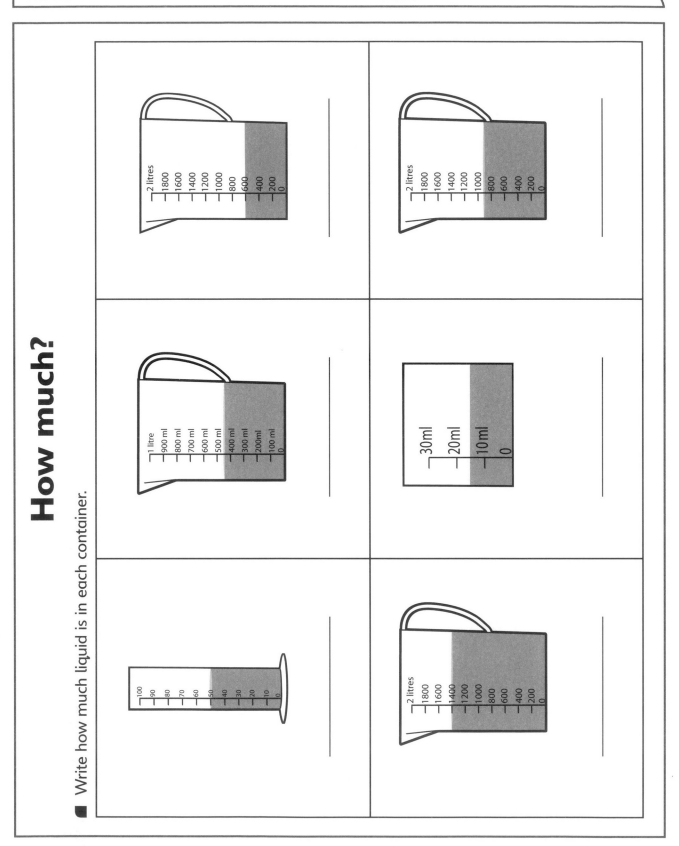

BLOCK C

How much?

Write how much liquid is in each container.

Dear Helper
This activity helps your child to read scales marked in millilitres and litres. If your child is unsure about how to read these, ask them to say how the scale is marked, what the start mark is, and how the scale increases. Ask them to look at the closest mark to the level of the liquid and to read this, then to make any adjustment if the liquid is above this. Challenge your child to fill a litre jug marked in millilitres to the level that you say.

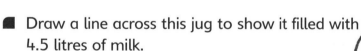
Name	Date

Jugs of milk

■ For each jug below, read the scale and write how much milk is in it.

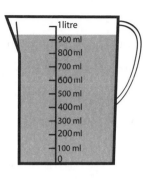

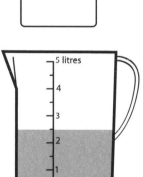

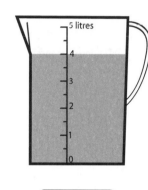

■ Draw a line across this jug to show it filled with 4.5 litres of milk.

Dear Helper

This activity helps your child to read scales marked in millilitres and litres. It gives an ideal opportunity to put theory into practice! In the kitchen, ask your child to fill a measuring jug with differing amounts of water. Start with an easy-to-read amount and then challenge them to be exact to the nearest 10ml.

BLOCK C

Name   Date

Which video game?

- Vince did a class survey about favourite types of video games.
- Here are the results of his survey:

  Six children like platform games.

  Nine children prefer racing games.

  Three children like puzzle games.

  15 children say sports games are their favourite.

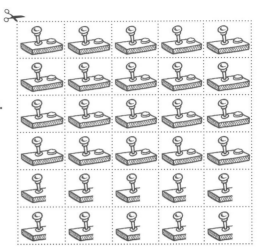

- Present Vince's results as a pictogram.

- Use  to show every two children.

- Use  to show one child.

Video game	Number of children
platform	
racing	
puzzle	
sports	

1. Which is the least popular style of video game? _____

2. Which is the most popular? _____

3. How many children did Vince ask altogether? _____

Dear Helper
This activity encourages your child to think about how information is displayed in tables, grids and graphs. Cut out the icons provided at the top of the page and help your child to stick the appropriate number into each row in the grid. If your child is unsure how many icons to use, explain that a whole joystick represents two children, and they will need to divide the number of children by 2 to work out how many whole and half joysticks to use for each video game.

Calculating, measuring and understanding shape

Activity name	Learning objectives	Managing the homework
D1		
Telling the time Write analogue time using digital format and answer some time questions.	Read the time on a 12-hour digital clock and to the nearest five minutes on an analogue clock; calculate time intervals	**Before:** Remind the children how to count around the clock face in five-minute intervals. **After:** Review the children's answers, particularly those at the bottom of the sheet. Invite the children to work out how long they sleep each night from their answers.
Holiday map Plot items using coordinates.	Read and record the vocabulary of position, direction and movement	**Before:** Check that the children are confident with the convention for writing coordinates. **After:** Review the work together using an A3 enlargement of the sheet. Invite individual children to show where each item belongs.
What's the time? Draw hands on clock faces to show analogue times for written digital times.	Read the time on a 12-hour digital clock and to the nearest five minutes on an analogue clock; calculate time intervals	**Before:** Suggest to the children that they may find it helpful to use a clock with hands to ensure that they draw in the hands accurately. **After:** Mark the homework together and discuss any issues that arose for the children while doing this homework.
Number patterns Continue addition and subtraction number patterns.	Add or subtract mentally combinations of one-digit and two-digit numbers	**Before:** Write up 54 − 5, then 54 − 15, and so on. Ask the children to say the answers and what comes next. **After:** Mark the homework together. Check that the children have understood the patterns and can continue them.
D2		
Find it! Describe a route using the four compass points.	Read and record the vocabulary of position, direction and movement, using the four compass directions to describe movement about a grid	**Before:** Remind the children of the four points of the compass and how to describe directions. **After:** Review the homework together, and discuss the various solutions that the children have found.
What's the problem? Calculate answers to number sentences and write a problem that will fit a given number sentence.	Represent the information in a puzzle or problem using numbers, images or diagrams; use these to find a solution and present it in context, where appropriate using £.p notation	**Before:** Discuss the strategies that children could use to solve number problems, including mental strategies, and using paper and pencil to help. **After:** Review the sheet together as the children mark their work. Invite suggestions for the word problems and discuss their suitability.
Money totals Find the total price of three items, with each price less than £1.	Add or subtract mentally combinations of one-digit and two-digit numbers	**Before:** Discuss how several amounts of money can be totalled by, for example, looking for pairs to make £1. **After:** Discuss the addition sentences that the children made and the strategies that they used for totalling.
Mirror, mirror Find and draw lines of symmetry in rectangles.	Draw and complete shapes with reflective symmetry; draw the reflection of a shape in a mirror line along one side	**Before:** Use a mirror to demonstrate and revise reflective symmetry. **After:** Review the homework. Use the sheet as an OHT and invite children to draw the lines of symmetry/reflections along the mirror lines.

Calculating, measuring and understanding shape

Activity name	Learning objectives	Managing the homework
D3		
Remainder search Find which divisors into a given number leave remainders.	Use practical and informal written methods to support multiplication and division of two-digit numbers (for example, 13 × 3, 30 ÷ 4)	**Before:** Ask division questions that result in remainders, such as 25 ÷ 4. **After:** Review the children's findings. Check that they have found which divisors into 24 leave a remainder and what the remainders are.
TV times Find start and end times in time interval problems.	Find start or end times for a given time interval	**Before:** Suggest to the children that they may find it helpful to use a clock face to count forward/back. **After:** Mark the homework together. Invite the children to explain how they arrived at the correct answers.
Think of a number Calculate the answers to multi-step number problems.	Use knowledge of number operations and corresponding inverses, including doubling and halving, to estimate and check calculations	**Before:** Read the first problem together. Explain how to tackle each step in turn to find the answer. **After:** Review the children's answers. Discuss whether they used the same strategy to find each answer.
Fill the jugs Read and mark scales for litres and millilitres.	Read, to the nearest division and half-division, scales that are numbered or partially numbered; use the information to measure and draw to a suitable degree of accuracy	**Before:** Remind the children how to read scales on containers. **After:** Mark the homework together, asking children from each ability group to give answers.

100 MATHS HOMEWORK ACTIVITIES · YEAR 3

■SCHOLASTIC

Name	Date

Telling the time

- Read the times on these clocks.
- Write the time in digital time. The first one has been done for you.

   6.10

   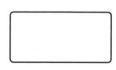

- Now answer these questions:

1. What time do you get up in the morning? _____

2. What time do you go to bed at night? _____

3. So how long are you out of bed during the day? _____

Dear Helper

This activity helps your child to read and write clock times. The times should be written in digital format. If your child is unsure about this, count together around a clock face, in five-minute intervals, to remind your child where the minute hand points. As a further challenge, ask your child to work out for how long they are asleep each night in a week... a month... a year!

BLOCK D

Name   Date

Holiday map

- This is an unfinished map of a camp site.
- Use the coordinates in the table to work out where the features belong on the map.
- Complete the map by drawing each feature in its square.

Item	Coordinate
Tents	(b, 2)
Toilet block	(c, 3)
Shop	(d, 4)
Car park	(c, 4)
Play area	(a, 3)
Swimming pool	(d, 5)
Restaurant	(e, 5)

BLOCK D

Dear Helper

This activity helps your child to locate positions on a grid. The convention is that the first letter or number represents the column and the second one the row. If your child is unsure about this, then plot one of the items together on the map, moving up the column and across the row until the two coordinates meet. Your child may like to add other things to the map and write a list of these and their coordinates.

Name   Date

What's the time?

◼ Read the time next to each clock.

◼ Draw in the hands to show that time on the clock.

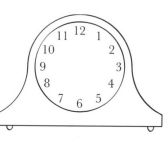 **3.00**    **6.30**

 **9.45**    **4.15**

 **10.05**    **8.20**

 **7.50**    **5.25**

 **1.35**    **11.40**

BLOCK D

Dear Helper

This activity helps your child to relate digital and analogue time. If your child finds it difficult to draw in the hands accurately, provide a clock with hands and ask them to set the time on it to match the digital time. Ask your child to describe where the hands are, then to draw the hands on the clock on this sheet. Challenge your child to be the timekeeper for a day, saying what the time is at regular intervals throughout the day.

Name	Date

Number patterns

■ Write the answers to these number sentences.

■ Continue the patterns.

16 + 8 = ☐

16 + 18 = ☐

16 + 28 = ☐

16 + ☐ = ☐

16 + ☐ = ☐

16 + ☐ = ☐

16 + ☐ = ☐

16 + ☐ = ☐

16 + ☐ = ☐

97 – 7 = ☐

97 – 17 = ☐

97 – 27 = ☐

97 – ☐ = ☐

97 – ☐ = ☐

97 – ☐ = ☐

97 – ☐ = ☐

97 – ☐ = ☐

97 – ☐ = ☐

24 + 7 = ☐

24 + 17 = ☐

24 + 27 = ☐

24 + ☐ = ☐

24 + ☐ = ☐

24 + ☐ = ☐

24 + ☐ = ☐

24 + ☐ = ☐

24 + ☐ = ☐

93 – 7 = ☐

93 – 17 = ☐

93 – 27 = ☐

93 – ☐ = ☐

93 – ☐ = ☐

93 – ☐ = ☐

93 – ☐ = ☐

93 – ☐ = ☐

93 – ☐ = ☐

Dear Helper

This activity helps your child to spot addition and subtraction patterns and to use these to help them to calculate. If your child is unsure, discuss what is happening. For example, if 16 + 8 = 24, then what is 16 + 18, 16 + 28, and so on. Discuss how the answer increases by 10 each time, as does the number that is added to 16. For the subtraction patterns, ask your child to explain what happens each time (reduces by 10 each time). Challenge your child to write their own addition and subtraction patterns.

Name   Date

Find it!

- Here is a plan of the park. Each little square is one step.

- Write the directions from the gate to the bench.

    ☐ Decide which way to go: north, south, east or west.

    ☐ Decide how many steps to take forward as you start off.

    ☐ Remember: you can only make right-angled turns.

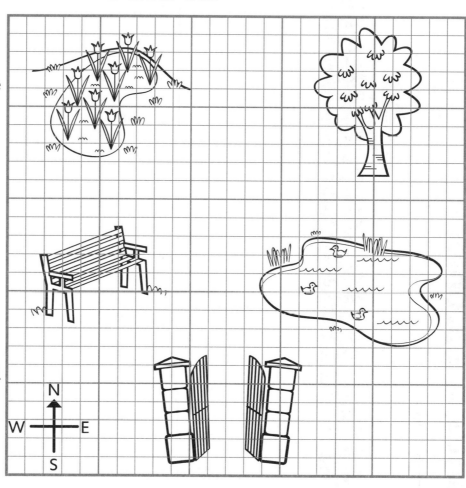

_____

_____

- Write directions from the bench to the tree.

_____

_____

- Now draw a statue in the park. Write directions from your statue back to the gate.

_____

_____

Dear Helper

This activity helps your child to recognise the points of the compass and encourages them to use right-angled turns when giving directions. If your child is unsure, trace the route from the gate to the bench with a pencil. Now discuss whether the movement is north, south, east or west. Count the number of steps forward. Discuss if a right-angled turn is needed. You could challenge your child to write directions for visiting everything in the park once, starting from the gate.

BLOCK D

Name

Date

BLOCK D

What's the problem?

- Write the answer to each number sentence.
- Now write a word problem to match each number sentence.

Number sentence	Answer	Word problem
36 + 15		
42 ÷ 5		
91 – 87		
☐ × 4	36	

Dear Helper

This activity helps your child to make decisions about which mathematics to use, and whether to use mental strategies or to make jottings as well. It also helps them to think about word problems involving numbers. If your child is unsure how to begin, discuss which mathematics will be needed and how this can be worked out. Then ask your child to put the numbers into a sentence to make a word problem. Challenge your child to write problems that also contain information that is not needed to help solve their problem.

Name _____ Date _____

Money totals

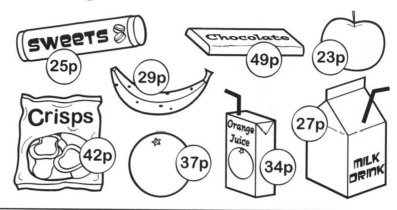

- Choose three different items from the shop.
- Find the total cost of the three items.
- Do this three more times.

I chose: _____

_____

_____

This cost _____

I chose: _____

_____

_____

This cost _____

I chose: _____

_____

_____

This cost _____

I chose: _____

_____

_____

This cost _____

BLOCK D

Dear Helper

This activity helps your child to choose strategies for totalling two-digit numbers. If necessary, remind your child to record their answer in pounds – 145 pence is the same as £1.45. If your child needs further help with this, provide some coins to help them. Extend this activity by challenging your child to total four or five prices each time.

Name	Date

Mirror, mirror

- ◣ A line of symmetry is like looking in a mirror. The halves of the shape on each side of the line must be the same, like a reflection.

- ◣ This rectangle (see right) has two lines of symmetry, while the triangle has only one line of symmetry.

- ◣ Draw the lines of symmetry in the shapes below.

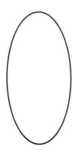  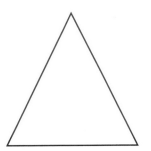 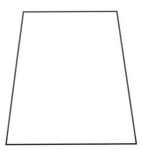

- ◣ Complete these shapes by drawing the reflection along the mirror line.

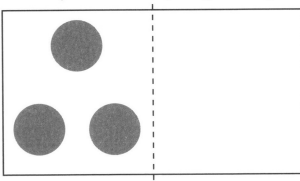 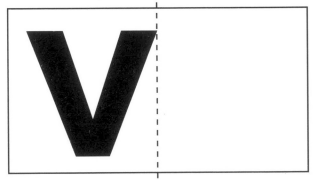

 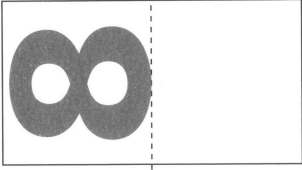

Dear Helper
This activity helps your child understand that reflective symmetry is like looking in a mirror; both sides of the shape should look exactly the same when looked at in a mirror along a line of symmetry. Reinforce their understanding by looking for lines of symmetry in pictures and lettering cut from old magazines. Draw the lines of symmetry onto the pictures using a felt-tipped pen. They also need to understand that some shapes don't have any lines of symmetry. You could challenge your child to find five examples of shapes that don't have any and five that have one or more lines of symmetry.

Name   Date

Remainder search

◾ Here are 24 ladybirds.

◾ Divide the ladybirds into groups of 2, 3, 4, 5 and 10.

◾ Find which division sums give remainders.

◾ Record your answers using the number sentences.

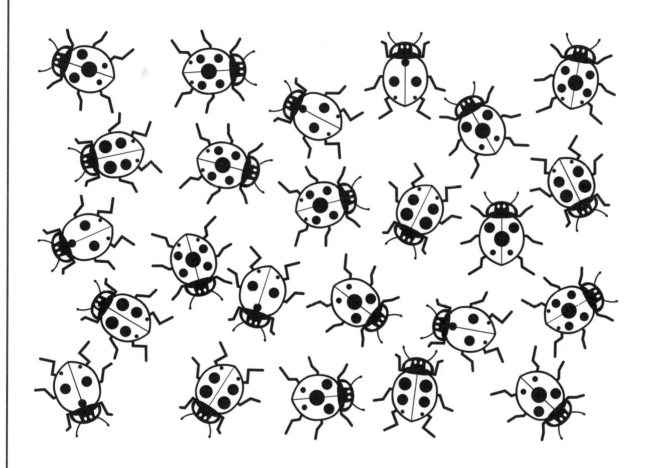

1. 24 ÷ 2 = _____   **2.** 24 ÷ 3 = _____

3. 24 ÷ 4 = _____   **4.** 24 ÷ 5 = _____

5. 24 ÷ 10 = _____

Dear Helper
This activity helps your child to use the multiplication table facts that they know to find division facts, and to identify where there is a remainder. If your child is unsure, say the appropriate multiplication table together until either the appropriate fact is found, or the nearest fact, then discuss what is 'left over', which will be the remainder. If your child would enjoy the challenge, ask them to divide 24 by 6, 7, 8 and 9 to see where there will be a remainder.

BLOCK D

Name	Date

TV times

- Trevor loves watching TV.
- Answer these questions about his viewing habits.

1. Trevor started watching *Motor Racing* at 6.30pm. The programme finished 45 minutes later. At what time did *Motor Racing* finish?

2. Trevor then watched *Cook it!* which ended 40 minutes before 9 o'clock. At what time did *Cook it!* end?

3. The news was on at 10 o'clock. Trevor fell asleep 25 minutes before it started. At what time did Trevor fall asleep?

4. Trevor woke up at 11.15pm! He watched *Late Night Chat* before going to bed. The programme started at 11.20pm and lasted half an hour. At what time did *Late Night Chat* end?

Dear Helper
This activity helps your child to find the start or end times for given time intervals. If your child is unsure about this, ask them to find the start time of the first programme on a clock face. Count together in five-minute intervals to find the programme's end time. For reinforcement, look at television listings in magazines and newspapers with your child. Ask each other questions about start and end times of your favourite programmes.

Name   Date

Think of a number

■ Try these puzzles which Magical Misty has set you.

■ Use a pencil to jot down notes.

1. I'm thinking of a number...
   I double it and take away 3.
   My answer is 11.
   What is my number?

2. I'm thinking of a number...
   I halve it and add 6.
   My answer is 14.
   What is my number?

3. I'm thinking of a number...
   I multiply it by 5 and add 10.
   My answer is 35.
   What is my number?

4. I'm thinking of a number...
   I divide it by 5 and take away 3.
   My answer is 3.
   What is my number?

BLOCK D

Dear Helper
This activity encourages your child to use their knowledge of number operations, including corresponding inverses, doubling and halving. If they are unsure how to start, look together at the first puzzle and work back from the answer. For example: 11 + 3 = 14 and 14 ÷ 2 = 7, so the starting number is 7. Challenge your child to make up three number puzzles such as these for you to answer. These puzzles are a really good way to improve mental maths skills.

Name   Date

Fill the jugs

■ Use the scales on the side of the jugs to read how much liquid is in each one.

■ Write the amounts underneath each jug.

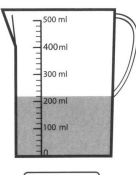 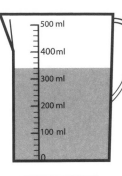 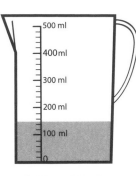 

■ Now fill these two jugs: 270ml in the first and 380ml in the second.

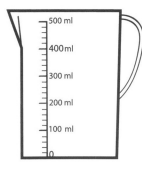 

Dear Helper

This activity helps your child to read and mark scales to a suitable level of accuracy. To reinforce this learning, challenge your child to measure amounts of water into a measuring jug. Encourage them to be accurate to the nearest millilitre. Fill the jug yourself and ask your child to read the scale.

Securing number facts, relationships and calculating

Activity name	Learning objectives	Managing the homework
E1		
Multiplication arrays Draw multiplication arrays and use equal addition.	Derive and recall multiplication facts for the 2-, 3-, 4-, 5- and 6-times tables	**Before:** Remind the children of an array, such as 5 × 3, by asking a child to make it with counters on the OHP. Then ask for the two equal addition sentences that could be made for that multiplication fact. **After:** Invite the children to demonstrate any further multiplications that they generated for themselves with counters and the OHP.
Division hops Divide by repeated subtraction along a number line.	● Derive and recall multiplication facts for the 2-, 3-, 4-, 5-, 6- and 10-times tables and the corresponding division facts ● Use practical and informal written methods to support multiplication and division of two-digit numbers (for example, 13 × 3, 50 ÷ 4)	**Before:** Using a counting stick, ask the children to practise counting back along the stick in threes, fours, fives and tens. **After:** Review the homework together. Check that the children understand that the jumps on the number line are repeated subtraction.
Wally the window cleaner Complete number sequences in steps of one, two, three, four, five and ten.	Derive and recall all addition and subtraction facts for each number to 20, sums and differences of 10 and number pairs that total 100	**Before:** Practise counting in steps of one, two, three, four, five and ten (forward and backward) using a number stick. **After:** Invite the children to suggest their own counting patterns in ones, twos, threes, fours, fives, and tens from and back to any small number.
Make 100 Calculate missing numbers in number sums totalling 100.	Derive and recall all addition and subtraction facts for each number to 20, sums and differences of 10 and number pairs that total 100	**Before:** Practise some quick-fire addition and subtraction, such as 50 + 20, 100 − 60 and so on. **After:** Mark the homework together. Ask the children to explain their strategy for calculating each missing number, ie total the two given numbers first.
Money problems Solve word problems involving multiplication and division of two-digit numbers.	Use practical and informal written methods to multiply and divide two-digit numbers (for example, 13 × 3, 50 ÷ 4)	**Before:** Practise some multiplication and division of two-digit numbers, such as 80 ÷ 4, 3 × 15 and so on. **After:** Review the homework together. Discuss whether the children used different strategies to solve the same problem.
Wheel fractions Shade fractions of a wheel and write equivalent fractions.	Find unit fractions of numbers and quantities (for example, $1/2$, $1/3$, $1/4$ and $1/6$ of 12 litres)	**Before:** Draw a wheel divided into six equal segments and ask: *How many segments would ½ be?* Check for other fractions. **After:** Review the work together and check that the children understand equivalent fractions (ie that $1/2$ is equal to $3/6$).
E2		
Fraction search Find the fraction to match the pictures.	Read and write proper fractions (for example, $3/7$, $9/10$), interpreting the denominator as the parts of a whole and the numerator as the number of parts; identify and estimate fractions of shapes	**Before:** Recap on unitary fractions, checking that children recognise that, for example, if $4/5$ is there, then the separate part is $1/5$. **After:** Review the homework together so that the children can mark their own. Invite children to say both fractions for each picture, such as $1/3$ and $2/3$.
Fraction shade Write the fractions of the shaded part of a variety of shapes.	Read and write proper fractions (for example, $3/7$, $9/10$), interpreting the denominator as the parts of a whole and the numerator as the number of parts; identify and estimate fractions of shapes	**Before:** Draw a 4 × 2 rectangular array and ask: *How many squares would $3/8$ be?* Check for other fractions. **After:** Invite the children to take turns to say the fraction for the shaded part, and the fraction of the unshaded part.

Securing number facts, relationships and calculating

Activity name	Learning objectives	Managing the homework
Double and halve Double a set of numbers, then halve the result.	Understand that division is the inverse of multiplication and vice versa; use to derive and record related multiplication and division sentences	**Before:** Practise some doubles, such as double 12, double 14 and so on. **After:** Ask the children to explain what happens when a number is doubled then halved.
Multiplication and division Use a known fact to find other facts for multiplication and division.	Understand that division is the inverse of multiplication and vice versa; use to derive and record related multiplication and division sentences	**Before:** Review some sets of multiplication and division facts, such as 5 × 3 = 15, 3 × 5 = 15, 15 ÷ 3 = 5 and 15 ÷ 5 = 3. **After:** Mark the homework together and discuss how a known multiplication or division fact helps us to find three other facts.
Multiples of 2, 5 and 10 Identify multiples in an array of numbers, and provide other examples of multiples.	Recognise multiples of 2, 5 or 10 up to 1000	**Before:** Ask: *How can we recognise a multiple of 2... 5... 10?* **After:** Mark the homework together, checking that the children have understood how to recognise these multiples.
Multiplying and dividing by 10 and 100 Quickly write the answers to multiplication and division by 10 and 100.	Multiply one-digit and two-digit numbers by 10 or 100, and describe the effect	**Before:** Ask: *What happens when we multiply by 10... 100?* **After:** Mark the homework together and check that the children understand what happens to the digits when they are multiplied by 10 or 100.
E3		
Number square challenge Find squares on the 100-square of four numbers and total opposite numbers.	Identify patterns and relationships involving numbers or shapes; use these to solve problems	**Before:** Explain the activity to the children, showing them how to identify a square of four numbers on the 100-square. **After:** Review the work together. Ask the children to explain their results.
How many? Solve a range of word problems.	Solve one-step and two-step problems involving numbers, money or measures, including time, choosing and carrying out appropriate calculations	**Before:** Discuss how to check an answer by using an equivalent calculation. **After:** Review the homework together. Invite children from each ability group to explain which check calculation they carried out, and why.
Tens and units multiplication Multiply the tens, then the digits, and add to find the answer.	Use practical and informal written methods to support multiplication and division of two-digit numbers (for example, 13 × 3, 50 ÷ 4)	**Before:** Remind the children of the strategy of combining the multiplication of the tens digit with the multiplication of the units digit to find the answer. **After:** Mark the homework together and check that the children have understood the strategy.
Column addition Use a column method to total HTU + TU.	Develop and use written methods to record, support or explain addition and subtraction of two-digit and three-digit numbers	**Before:** Remind the children of the school's method for column addition. **After:** Mark the homework together. Invite individual children to demonstrate on the board how they worked out the answers.
Make a number Use digit cards to make three-digit numbers.	Partition three-digit numbers into multiples of 100, 10 and 1 in different ways	**Before:** Remind the children of the value of each digit (H, T, U) in a three-digit number. **After:** Review the work together, and ask the children to explain their answers.
Out to lunch Solve a set of word problems using fractions of quantities.	Find unit fractions of quantities (for example, $\frac{1}{2}$, $\frac{1}{3}$, $\frac{1}{4}$ and $\frac{1}{6}$ of 12 litres)	**Before:** Recap on finding fractions of quantities. Ask: *What is ½ of 20? How did you work it out?* **After:** Review the homework together, asking children from each ability group to give answers.

■SCHOLASTIC

Name	Date

Multiplication arrays

- Read each multiplication sentence.
- Shade in the multiplication array. The first one has been done for you.
- Write the two equal addition sentences and the answer.

$4 \times 2 =$ ☐ = ☐ + ☐ = ☐ + ☐ + ☐

$5 \times 4 =$ ☐ = ☐ + ☐ + ☐ = ☐ + ☐ + ☐ + ☐

$6 \times 3 =$ ☐ = ☐ + ☐ + ☐ + ☐ + ☐ + ☐ = ☐ + ☐ + ☐

$7 \times 3 =$ ☐ = ☐ + ☐ + ☐ + ☐ + ☐ + ☐ + ☐ = ☐ + ☐ + ☐

BLOCK E

Dear Helper
This activity helps your child to understand that multiplication can be seen as a rectangle of small squares or counters and as equal addition. If your child is unsure, provide some counters, buttons or pennies, and ask them to try setting out a rectangle for 3×2. This can be set out as two rows of three or three rows of two. Then ask your child to write the additions: $3 + 3 = 6$, and $2 + 2 + 2 = 6$. If your child would enjoy a challenge, encourage them to write another five multiplications, drawing the arrays and writing the addition sentences on the back of this sheet.

Name	Date

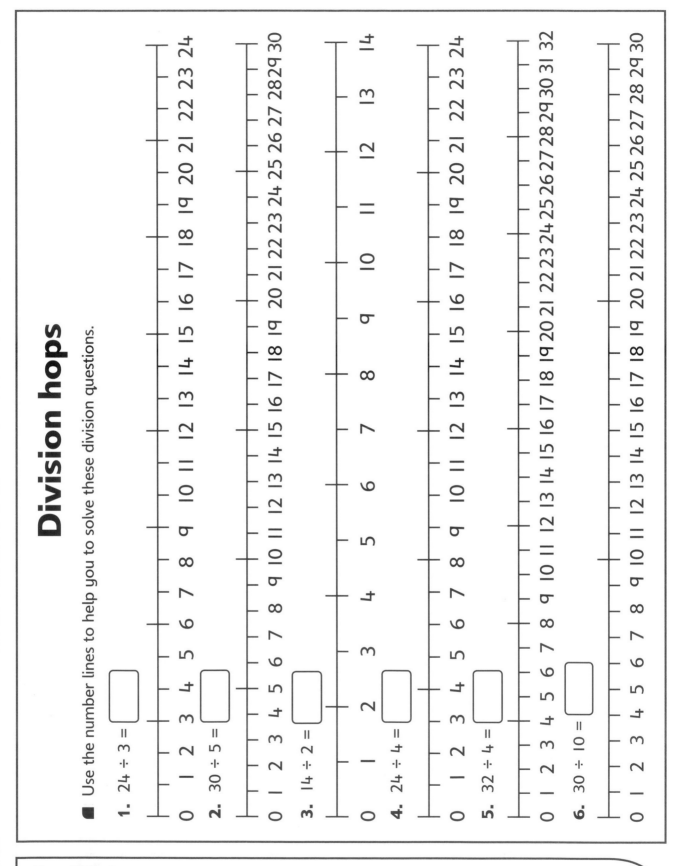

Division hops

■ Use the number lines to help you to solve these division questions.

1. 24 ÷ 3 = ▢

0 1 2 3 4 5 6 7 8 9 10 11 12 13 14 15 16 17 18 19 20 21 22 23 24

2. 30 ÷ 5 = ▢

0 1 2 3 4 5 6 7 8 9 10 11 12 13 14 15 16 17 18 19 20 21 22 23 24 25 26 27 28 29 30

3. 14 ÷ 2 = ▢

0 1 2 3 4 5 6 7 8 9 10 11 12 13 14

4. 24 ÷ 4 = ▢

0 1 2 3 4 5 6 7 8 9 10 11 12 13 14 15 16 17 18 19 20 21 22 23 24

5. 32 ÷ 4 = ▢

0 1 2 3 4 5 6 7 8 9 10 11 12 13 14 15 16 17 18 19 20 21 22 23 24 25 26 27 28 29 30 31 32

6. 30 ÷ 10 = ▢

0 1 2 3 4 5 6 7 8 9 10 11 12 13 14 15 16 17 18 19 20 21 22 23 24 25 26 27 28 29 30

Dear Helper

This activity helps your child to recognise that division can be seen as repeated subtraction. If they are unsure about how to begin the activity, they can count along the number line in hops. So, for 24 ÷ 3, they count how many 3s there are from 0 to 24, or they can count back along the line from 24 to 0. If appropriate, challenge your child to try some more difficult division questions, such as 48 ÷ 6 or 56 ÷ 8.

Name		Date	

Wally the window cleaner

◼ These number sequences have been ruined by Wally the window cleaner. He has wiped some of the numbers away with his wiper!

◼ Help Wally repair the damage and fill in the missing numbers.

2	5	8		14		20
1	4	7		13		19
5	7		11	13		
3	7		15			
4	9					
20	17		11			
20	18		14			
20	16			4		
20		10				
20	19					

Dear Helper
This activity helps your child to derive and recall addition and subtraction facts for numbers up to 20. If they are unsure how to begin, look at each sequence and ask them to count on/back from the first number to the second to work out the interval. As a challenge, give them a quick-fire quiz to increase the speed of their recall. Learning these facts will be a real aid to their mental arithmetic skills.

BLOCK E

Name	Date

Make 100

■ Which number is missing in each of Rio's trios of numbers?

20 + 30 + ☐ = 100

☐ + 40 + 30 = 100

10 + 70 + ☐ = 100

60 + ☐ + 20 = 100

50 + ☐ + 10 = 100

25 + 35 + ☐ = 100

15 + 45 + ☐ = 100

30 + ☐ + 5 = 100

26 + 51 + ☐ = 100

39 + ☐ + 33 = 100

Dear Helper
This activity asks your child to recall addition and subtraction facts to work out number sums that total 100. Encourage them to attempt these sums using their mental arithmetic skills, but if necessary, they can use a pencil and paper. If they are unsure how to start, show them how to add the two given numbers first in order then subtract the total from 100 to work out the missing number.

BLOCK E

Name	Date

Money problems

◀ Use a pencil and paper to work out these word problems.

Sanjev has saved four 10p coins. How much does he have in total?	Fiona has 60p in 10p coins. How many coins does she have?	Leo spends 70p on ten sweets. How much does each sweet cost?	Rina buys five bangles which cost 15p each. How much does she spend altogether?
James spends 90p on ten toy soldiers. How much does each toy soldier cost?	Jamelia has five 20p coins. How much money does she have in total?	Jed buys five custard tarts costing 30p each. How much does Jed spend?	Georgina spent 80p on two cans of drink. How much does each can cost?

Dear Helper
This activity helps your child to solve word problems using informal written methods to multiply and divide two-digit numbers. If they are unsure how to start, discuss how to translate the information into a sum. For example: four 10p coins = 4 × 10p = 40p. Encourage your child to use this thought process and to explain how they solved each problem. At school, your child is taught to partition numbers when doing calculations. For example, the calculation 14 × 3 is partitioned as: (10 × 3) + (4 × 3) = 30 + 12 = 42.

Name	Date

Wheel fractions

■ These wheels are all divided into 12 equal segments.

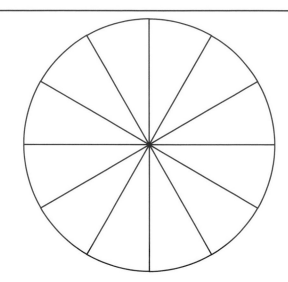

Shade in one half of this wheel.

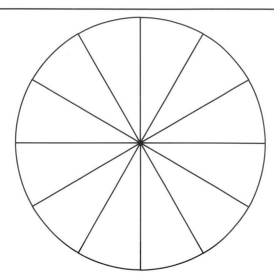

Shade in one third of this wheel.

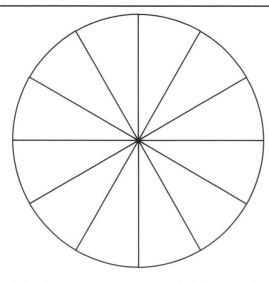

Shade in one quarter of this wheel.

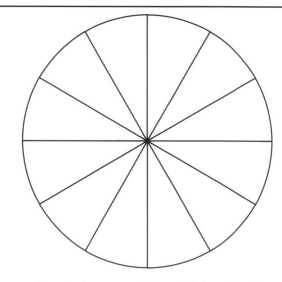

Shade in one sixth of this wheel.

■ Equivalent means 'the same as'.

1. How many sixths are equivalent to one half? _____

2. How many sixths are equivalent to one third? _____

3. How many quarters are equivalent to one half? _____

Dear Helper

This activity helps your child to find unit fractions of numbers and equivalent fractions. If they are unsure, explain that the bottom number of the fraction tells you how many parts the shape is divided into and the top number of the fraction tells you how many parts to colour in. If your child is confident finding $^1/_3$ or $^1/_6$ of a shape, challenge them to find $^2/_3$ or $^5/_6$ of a shape.

BLOCK E

Name   Date

Fraction search

◼ Draw a line to join each picture to its corresponding fraction.

$\frac{1}{10}$

$\frac{1}{8}$

$\frac{1}{4}$

$\frac{1}{2}$

$\frac{1}{3}$

BLOCK E

Dear Helper
This activity helps your child to recognise the fractions $\frac{1}{2}$, $\frac{1}{3}$, $\frac{1}{4}$, $\frac{1}{8}$, and $\frac{1}{10}$. If your child is unsure, ask:
How many pieces are there altogether? So this one [pointing to the one that is separate] *is what fraction?*
Challenge your child to say both fractions for each picture. For example, the pizza shows $\frac{2}{3}$ and $\frac{1}{3}$.

Name	Date

Fraction shade

Write the fraction for the shaded part of each shape.

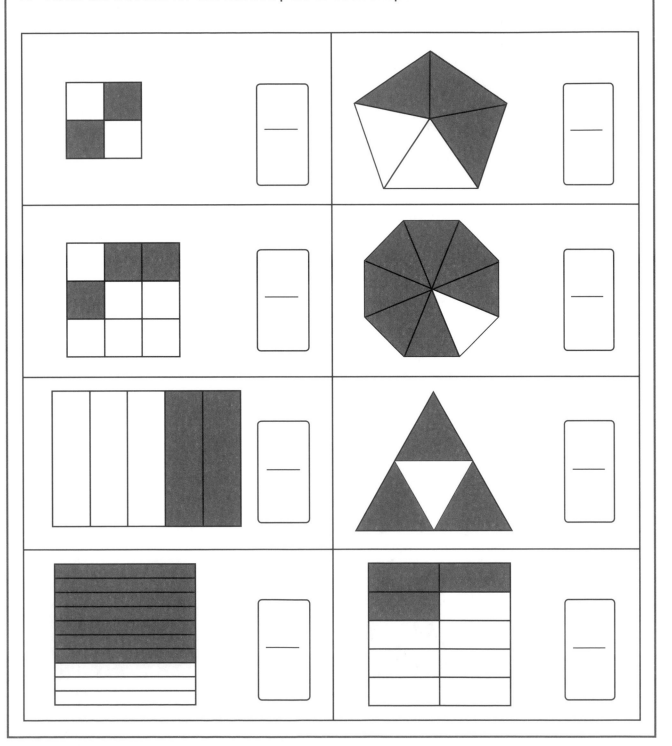

Dear Helper
This activity helps your child to recognise fractions of shapes that are several parts of a whole. If your child is unsure, ask them to count how many parts there are altogether. This will give the denominator (bottom number) of the fraction. Now ask your child to count how many are shaded. This gives the numerator (top number) of the fraction. So, for 8 parts in all and 7 shaded, the fraction is $^7/_8$. Challenge your child to draw some sets of spots, separate some with a ring, and write the fraction of the separated set.

PHOTOCOPIABLE **■**SCHOLASTIC

Name	Date

Double and halve

◼ Write the double of each number in the first box.

◼ Now write half of that number in the second box.

☐ The first one has been done for you.

20 ⟶ [40] ⟶ [20]

15 ⟶ [ ] ⟶ [ ]

14 ⟶ [ ] ⟶ [ ]

9 ⟶ [ ] ⟶ [ ]

18 ⟶ [ ] ⟶ [ ]

16 ⟶ [ ] ⟶ [ ]

◼ Now try these.

12 × 2 = [ ]   24 ÷ 2 = [ ]

13 × 2 = [ ]   26 ÷ 2 = [ ]

17 × 2 = [ ]   34 ÷ 2 = [ ]

19 × 2 = [ ]   38 ÷ 2 = [ ]

◼ Write two of these doubling and halving sums for yourself.

[ ] × 2 = [ ]   [ ] ÷ 2 = [ ]

[ ] × 2 = [ ]   [ ] ÷ 2 = [ ]

BLOCK E

Dear Helper

This activity helps your child to make the link between doubling and halving, and to recognise that division is the inverse, or opposite, of multiplication. If your child finds this difficult, double the tens digit, then the units digit and add the results in order to find the double. For halving, ask: *What do we double to make 34? Yes, 17. So half of 34 is 17.* Challenge your child to write some more difficult number sentences like these.

Name	Date

Multiplication and division

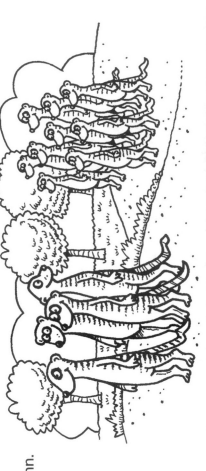

- Write the answer to the first multiplication question.
- Use the same numbers to write another multiplication sentence in the second column.
- Now use the same numbers to write two division sentences in the third and fourth columns.
- Now fill in the rest of the table, using the numbers that are given to you.
  □ The last set has been done for you.

Multiplication	Multiplication	Division	Division
5 × 4 =			
6 × 3 =		24 ÷ 3 =	
		30 ÷ 5 =	
9 × 10 =			
9 × 4 = 36	4 × 9 = 36	36 ÷ 4 = 9	36 ÷ 9 = 4

Dear Helper

This activity helps your child to recognise that if they know one multiplication or division fact then they can work out three other facts. If your child is unsure about how to begin, discuss which multiplication table the numbers belong to. Encourage your child to say the multiplication table to find the fact. Extend this activity by challenging your child to write some more linked facts like these.

Name   Date

Multiples of 2, 5 and 10

◼ See how quickly you can do this activity. Time how long it takes.

1. Circle the multiples of 2 in this set of numbers.

1   4   9   18   36   45   88   102   654   748

2. Circle the multiples of 5 in this set of numbers.

5   12   25   41   52   65   80   315   450   900

3. Circle the multiples of 10 in this set of numbers.

9   20   47   80   95   100   120   231   845   870

4. Write the list of unit digits that tell you that a number is a multiple of 2.

_____

5. Write the list of unit digits that tell you that a number is a multiple of 5.

_____

6. How you can tell that a number is a multiple of 10?

_____

_____

7. Write three numbers which are each a multiple of 2, 5 and 10.

_____

◼ I took ☐ minutes to do this homework activity.

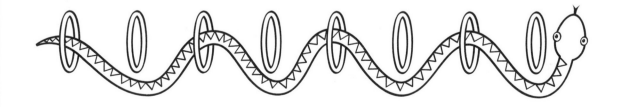

Dear Helper
This activity helps your child to use the rules for recognising multiples of 2, 5 and 10. If your child is unsure, take each number in the list at a time, and ask your child to decide whether it will come in the count of 2s... 5s... 10s. Challenge your child to write a list of numbers that are *not* multiples of 2, 5 or 10.

BLOCK E

Name	Date

Multiplying and dividing by 10 and 100

◾ Write the answers to these questions.

☐ See how quickly you can do this. Time how long it takes.

3 × 10 = ☐

7 × 100 = ☐

25 × 10 = ☐

5 × 100 = ☐

60 ÷ 10 = ☐

500 ÷ 100 = ☐

800 ÷ 10 = ☐

900 ÷ 100 = ☐

40 ÷ 10 = ☐

8 × 100 = ☐

◾ I took ☐ minutes to do this homework activity.

Dear Helper

This activity helps your child to recognise that when multiplying by 10 the digits shift one place to the left and when mulitplying by 100 they shift two places to the left. When dividing by 10 the digits shift one place to the right; when dividing by 100 they shift two places to the right. If your child is unsure, discuss whether it is a division or multiplication question and which way the digits will shift. Challenge your child to work quickly and accurately.

BLOCK E

Name   Date

Number square challenge

- Look at the number grid. The four numbers 1, 2, 11 and 12 make a small number square.

1	2	3	4	5	6	7	8	9	10
11	12	13	14	15	16	17	18	19	20
21	22	23	24	25	26	27	28	29	30
31	32	33	34	35	36	37	38	39	40
41	42	43	44	45	46	47	48	49	50

- Add opposite numbers like this:

    $1 + 12 = 13$

    $2 + 11 = 13$

- Now choose your own four numbers that make a small square.
    - ☐ Draw a square around your numbers on the number grid.
    - ☐ Add opposite numbers.
    - ☐ Do this three more times.

I chose [   ] [   ] [   ] [   ]   I chose [   ] [   ] [   ] [   ]

[   ] + [   ] = [   ]   [   ] + [   ] = [   ]

[   ] + [   ] = [   ]   [   ] + [   ] = [   ]

I chose [   ] [   ] [   ] [   ]   I chose [   ] [   ] [   ] [   ]

[   ] + [   ] = [   ]   [   ] + [   ] = [   ]

[   ] + [   ] = [   ]   [   ] + [   ] = [   ]

- What do you notice about your results?
- Write some sentences on the back of this sheet to explain your results.

BLOCK E

Dear Helper

This activity encourages your child to think about why opposite numbers in a number square make equal totals. If your child finds this difficult, break each number down into tens and units. So, for the square 1, 2, 11 and 12, the opposite numbers 1 and 12 contain 1 + 10 + 2, and the opposite numbers 2 and 11 contain 2 + 10 + 1. Each total contains the same digits, but not in the same order. Challenge your child to choose larger squares, such as a 3 × 3 square, total opposite corner numbers and describe their results.

Name	Date

How many?

■ Write the answer to each problem.

　☐ There is space for jottings.

■ Now write a check calculation to check your answer.

Problem and answer	Jottings	Check calculation
Jaminda buys some fruit for her class. There are 25 children in the class and each child has two pieces of fruit. There are 12 pieces of fruit left over. How many pieces of fruit did Jaminda buy? ☐		
Peter helps his mum to wash the dishes every evening. He spends nine minutes each evening doing this. How long does he spend washing dishes during one week? ☐ minutes		
Sarah always brings an apple to school to eat at break. In July there were only three whole weeks and three days at school. So how many apples did she need in July? ☐		

Dear Helper

This activity helps your child to decide which mathematics to use to solve a problem, and then to check with an equivalent calculation. If your child finds this difficult, talk through the problem. Decide what the question is asking, and which information is needed to solve the problem. Discuss which mathematics to use. To check, ask your child to suggest another way of working out the problem. Challenge them to find more than one way to check the answer to each problem.

BLOCK E

Name	Date

Tens and units multiplication

■ This is a way to calculate 32 × 2:

    30 × 2 = 60

     2 × 2 = 4

    So 32 × 2 = 60 + 4 = 64

■ Now try this method for these multiplication sentences.

43 × 2	23 × 2
24 × 3	48 × 2
14 × 3	26 × 4

BLOCK E

Dear Helper

This activity helps your child to use a method for multiplication of tens and units by units. If your child is unsure, follow the example given above and work through each question, multiplying the tens digit first, then the units, then combining the two to find the answer. To extend the activity, challenge your child to write five more of these questions for themselves and see how quickly they can find the answers.

Name   Date

Column addition

- ◼ Work out the answers to each of these questions using two different methods.
- ◼ Use a horizontal method first.
- ◼ Then use the column addition method that you were taught at school.
- ◼ Write the answer.
- ◼ Check that both methods give the same answer.

246 + 87 = ☐	2 4 6 + 8 7
545 + 78 = ☐	5 4 5 + 7 8
298 + 79 = ☐	2 9 8 + 7 9

BLOCK E

Dear Helper
Your child has been taught a method of column addition at school. Ask them to explain this to you. It may not be the method that you were taught, but please help your child to do these in the way that they have been taught at school. By working out each question using two different methods of setting out the addition sentence, your child is learning that both methods give the same answer, and that the way of working is similar. Challenge your child to do these quickly and efficiently.

Name	Date

Make a number

◾ Akram has three cards.

1. Using all three cards, what is the largest number Akram can make?

_____

2. What is the smallest three-digit number he can make?

_____

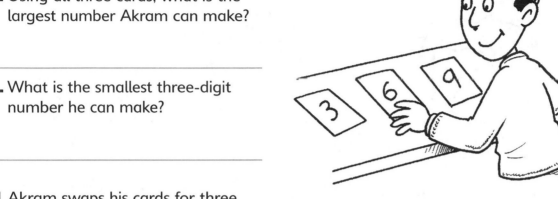

◾ Akram swaps his cards for three different ones.

3. Using all three cards, what is the largest number he can make now?

_____

4. What is the smallest three-digit number he can make?

_____

◾ Akram now takes both sets of cards.

5. Using three different cards, what is the largest three-digit number he can make?

_____

6. What is the smallest three-digit number he can make?

_____

BLOCK E

Dear Helper
This activity helps your child to understand the partitioning of three-digit numbers into multiples of 100, 10 and 1. If they are unsure, write the headings H, T and U and discuss how the digits have a different value, depending on which heading they sit under. Make a set of digit cards 1–9 and investigate making different three-digit numbers with your child. Ask: _How much is each digit is worth in this number?_ For example, 492 is 400 + 90 + 2. Deal out the cards equally and see who can make the largest number first.

Name	Date

Out to lunch

◼ Gordon went out for lunch with his friends.

◼ The bill came to £30.

1. One half of the bill was for burgers. How much was spent on burgers?

2. One third of the bill was spent on milkshakes. How much was this?

3. One sixth of the bill was spent on ice cream. How much was this?

4. To get home, Gordon spent a quarter of a £20 note on a taxi.
How much was the taxi fare?

Dear Helper
This activity asks your child to find unit fractions of numbers and quantities. If they are unsure how to begin, look at the first question and discuss how to represent this work problem as a fraction sum. For example: *What is ½ of £30?* As reinforcement, your child can practise finding fractions of money using coins. Gather together some loose change and challenge them to find halves, quarters, thirds and sixths of 20p, 30p and 60p.

Puzzles and problems: Objectives grid

The puzzles and problems activities can be used very flexibly to provide children with fun maths tasks to take home. The puzzles and problems are based on work that children will be covering during the year and should test their use and application of mathematics at an appropriate level. Where possible, children should be encouraged to try different approaches to solving these problems and to look for clues and patterns in mathematics.

The grid below lists each activity and identifies links to the different objectives within the Using and applying mathematics strand of the Renewed Framework.

	Solve one-step and two-step problems involving numbers, money or measures, including time, choosing and carrying out appropriate calculations	Represent the information in a puzzle or problem using numbers, images or diagrams; use these to find a solution and present it in context, where appropriate using £.p notation or units of measure	Follow a line of enquiry by deciding what information is important; make and use lists, tables and graphs to organise and interpret the information	Identify patterns and relationships involving numbers or shapes, and use these to solve problems	Describe and explain methods, choices and solutions to puzzles and problems, orally and in writing, using pictures and diagrams
1 What's in the box?	✔				
2 Election selection	✔				
3 Busker Gus	✔				
4 MC Squared	✔				
5 Time flies	✔				
6 Savour the flavours	✔				
7 Circle skills				✔	
8 Who am I?				✔	
9 Rope trick	✔				
10 How many wheels?	✔				
11 Let's operate	✔				
12 Mirror, mirror...				✔	
13 Who ate the pie?				✔	
14 Who's wrong?	✔				
15 Right-angle hunt				✔	
16 Fishy fun!	✔				
17 Puzzle rings			✔		
18 Sunshine Sue		✔			
19 Dozy Dizzy!	✔				
20 My slug's bigger!		✔			
21 Sally's tally chart					✔
22 Go digital!	✔				
23 Bouncing baby	✔				
24 Weigh it up	✔				
25 Letter change				✔	
26 Christmas shopping	✔				
27 Orange juice	✔				
28 What comes next?				✔	
29 What's my number?	✔				
30 Who's the heaviest?	✔				
31 In the sale	✔				
32 What's in the tank?			✔		
33 Wolf pack		✔			
34 Same as?	✔				
35 Witch's teeth					✔
36 Football stickers	✔				

1 What's in the box?

Marco the Magician has hidden a number in this calculation. What number has he hidden?

2 Election selection

These are the results of the school council election.

Ray Gunn: 274 votes

Bella Rings: 427 votes

Neal Down: 342 votes

Stan Dupp: 234 votes

Penny Chews: 324 votes

Write the correct finishing order, starting with the winner first.

_____

_____

_____

_____

_____

Puzzles and problems

3 Busker Gus

Busker Gus has finished busking for the day.

How much money does he have in his guitar case?

4 MC Squared

Rapper MC Squared bought a pair of trainers in the sale for £2.29. He paid with two £2 coins.

How much change did he get?

5 Time flies

Scarlett started her homework at 6.20pm and was having so much fun she carried on for 40 minutes.

She went to bed an hour later.

What time did Scarlett go to bed?

6 Savour the flavours

Luigi had 32 flavours of ice cream but he left nine of them out of the freezer and they melted.

How many flavours did Luigi have left?

7 Circle skills

Draw a ring around the shape in
this circle which is half a circle.

8 Who am I?

I am a two-digit number
whose digits total 8 and
have a difference of 6.

Which two numbers could I
be?

9 Rope trick

Raj's rope is one metre long.

He cuts off eight lots of 5cm pieces to do a magic trick.

How long is his piece of rope now?

10 How many wheels?

Dave has nine cars.

How many wheels does he have altogether?

How many wheels does he have if you include steering wheels?

PHOTOCOPIABLE **■SCHOLASTIC**

11 **Let's operate**

Doctor Proctor multiplies
6 by 7 to make 42.

What operation will turn
42 back into 6?

_____

12 **Mirror, mirror...**

Draw the mirror reflection
to complete this face.

13 Who ate the pie?

Roughly how much of this
pie has been eaten?

_____

14 Who's wrong?

Two of these children are talking nonsense. Circle them.

38 is divisible by 6, don't you know?

4 lots of 9 make 36, I tell you!

Of course, 34 divided by 5 equals 12.

15 Right-angle hunt

How many right angles can you
find inside this shape?

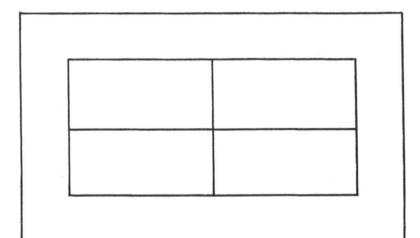

16 Fishy fun!

Angie the angler has caught
three beauties!

How long are these fish?

_____

_____

_____

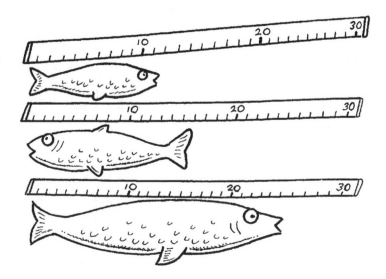

17 Puzzle rings

Sven has been given the numbers 1 to 20, and told to write them in the Venn diagram.

In the left ring go even numbers and in the right ring go the multiples of 5.

Some numbers could go in both rings. They go in the middle.

In the area outside the rings, write all the numbers that don't match either category.

Help Sven complete the diagram.

18 Sunshine Sue

Sue wants to go somewhere warm for her holiday.

Write the temperature of each holiday place.

Sue wants to go to the warmest place.

Where should she go?

_____

_____

_____

_____

_____

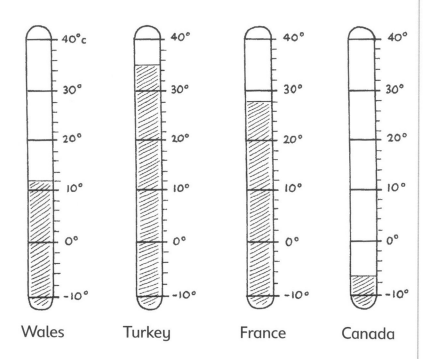

Wales   Turkey   France   Canada

Puzzles and problems

19 Dozy Dizzy!

Dizzy has slept in again and is late for school!

He set off at five to nine and got to school at twenty to ten.

How long did it take Dizzy to get to school?

20 My slug's bigger!

Jess found a slug that was 9cm long.

Caitlin found one which was 3cm bigger but it slipped away!

How long was Caitlin's slug?

Use a ruler to draw Caitlin's slug to the correct length here.

21 Sally's tally chart

Sally did a survey of how her friends travelled to school.

She needs your help to complete her tally chart.

Fill in the empty boxes.

Transport	Number of children	Frequency
Scooter	7	
Walk		⦀⦀ |||
Bike	4	
Car		⦀⦀	

22 Go digital!

Auntie Edith is going digital!

She wants to know the difference in time between her old clock and the digital one.

Write your answer in minutes.

Puzzles and problems

23 **Bouncing baby**

Matthew has just been born.

The nurse has just weighed him.

Circle the weight you think he is.

15kg

23g

2 tonnes

3kg

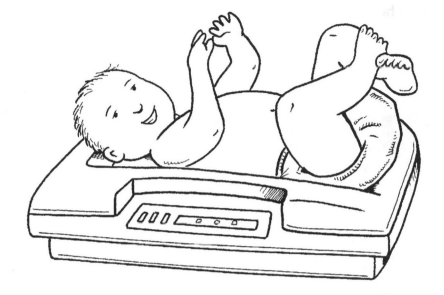

24 **Weigh it up**

Jamie puts 85g of flour into one pan of his kitchen balance and 35g of flour into the other.

How much flour does he have to add to the 35g to make it balance?

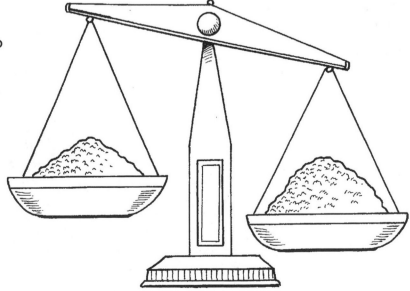

25 Letter change

If the letter 'd' is reflected on its straight line it turns into a different letter.

Which letter does it become?

_____

26 Christmas shopping

Dad has been Christmas shopping.

He bought a necklace for Mum for £8.49 and a box of chocolates for Gran for £3.42.

How much did Dad spend altogether?

_____

Puzzles and problems

27 Orange juice

Kim has squeezed some fresh
orange juice.

How much juice is in the jug?

[ ]

1000 ml

800 ml

600 ml

400 ml

200 ml

28 What comes next?

Frankie has written a
number pattern but his little
sister has rubbed out two of
the numbers.

What are the missing two
numbers?

14   17   –   23   26   –

[ ]   [ ]

29 What's my number?

I have three numbers that add up to 100 under these pots.

Here are two of them. What number is still hidden?

30 Who's the heaviest?

Tom is $\frac{1}{2}$ the weight of Dom, who is 48kg.

Beth is $\frac{3}{4}$ the weight of Steph, who is 36kg.

Who is heavier, Tom or Beth?

_____

How much heavier is that person?

_____

Puzzles and problems

31 In the sale

Last year's summer dress cost £60.

It has $\frac{1}{3}$ taken off the price in the sale.

What is the new price of the dress?

32 What's in the tank?

Lewis needs $\frac{3}{4}$ of a tank of petrol to complete the race. This is how much he has.

Approximately how full is the tank?

Will he be able to complete the race without filling up with more petrol?

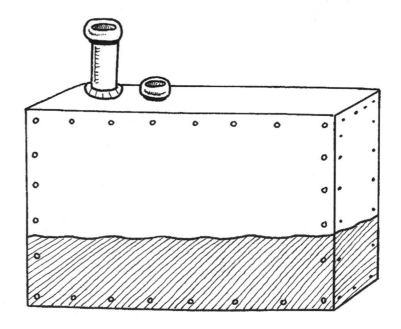

33 **Wolf pack**

There are 36 legs in a wolf pack.

How many wolves are there?

34 **Same as?**

Write the number that is the same as:

300 + 120 + 9

35 Witch's teeth

Wicked witch Wanda wants half of her teeth to be rotten.

At the moment she only has three rotten teeth!

Shade in the remainder to give her half of a rotten set.

36 Football stickers

Wayne has $\frac{1}{3}$ of 60 stickers and Theo has $\frac{1}{5}$ of 50 stickers.

How many stickers do Wayne and Theo have each?

Wayne

Theo

Block A

P9 **Number match** Answers for the second part will vary

P10 **Partitioning** 600, 40, 9; 300, 30, 3; 500, 0, 9; 500, 90, 0; 900, 50, 0; 900, 0, 5; 200, 30, 7. Answers for the second part will vary

P11 **Counting patterns** Answers will vary

P12 **Number order** 156, 165, 516, 561, 615, 651; 831, 879, 887, 897, 901, 910; 497, 499, 500, 501, 504, 516. Answers to the second part will vary

P13 **Addition** 55; 84; 69; 79; 88; 93; 51; 97; 83; 101

P14 **Times 10 and 100** 50, 500; 80, 800; 40, 400; 90, 900; 70, 700; 10, 100; 100, 1000; 300, 3000; 800, 8000; 900, 9000

P15 **Race track challenge** Answers will vary

P16 **Add these** 24; 25; 26; 32; 37; 33; 37; 41; 41; 36. Answers to the second part will vary

P17 **Find the difference** 3; 6; 4; 6; 6; 5; 5; 7; 9; 4

P18 **Adding and adjusting** 45 (+ 19) 64; 65 (+ 21) 86; 56 (+ 19) 75; 57 (+ 29) 86; 52 (+ 21) 73; 34 (+ 29) 63; 69 (+ 31) 100; 28 (+ 21) 49; 29 (+ 29) 58; 62 (+ 19) 81

P19 **Add and subtract** 81, 152, 171, 180, 237, 37, 17, 35, 88, 245

P20 **Division problems** 4; 9; 6, £30; 5

Block B

P23 **Is it true?** The sentence 'All squares are rectangles.' is true. Answers will vary

P24 **Odd numbers** Answers will vary

P25 **Find the change** 20p – 16p = 4p; 50p – 16p = 34p; £1 – 16p = 84p; £2 – 16p = £1.84

P26 **Presents** Answers will vary

P27 **Check it** 64; 76; 37; 29; 30; 87; 97; 36; 49; 87

P28 **Making shapes**

Cutting one right angle:

Cutting two right angles:

P29 **Money puzzle** The different combinations are: 20p + 20p + 20p = 60p; 20p + 20p + 50p = 90p; 20p + 50p + 50p = £1.20; 50p + 50p + 50p = £1.50; 20p + 20p + £1 = £1.40; 20p + £1 + £1 = £2.20; £1 + £1 + £1 = £3; 20p + 20p + £2 = £2.40; 20p + £2 + £2 = £4.20; £2 + £2 + £2 = £6; 50p + 50p + £1 = £2; 50p + £1 + £1 = £2.50; 50p + 50p + £2 = £3; 50p + £2 + £2 = £4.50; £1 + £1 + £2 = £4; £1 + £2 + £2 = £5; £1 + 20p + 50p = £1.70; 20p + 50p + £2 = £2.70; £2 + 50p + £1 = £3.50; £2 + £1 + 20p = £3.20

P30 **Odds and evens** Answers will vary

P31 **Sticker problems** 65; 50; 40, 57; 57

P32 **Equivalent fractions** $^2/_8$, $^1/_4$; $^4/_{10}$, $^2/_5$; $^4/_6$, $^2/_3$; $^8/_{10}$, $^4/_5$; $^5/_{10}$, $^1/_2$

P33 **Fraction match** No answers

P34 **Is it symmetrical?** Lines of symmetry:

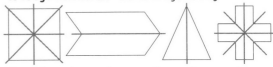

The other shapes have no lines of symmetry.

P35 **Sorting 2D shapes**

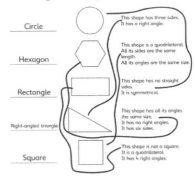

P36 **Calculation check** 71; 7; 5; 32; 19

P37 **Measures word problems** 900ml or 0.9 litres or $^9/_{10}$ litre; 1350g or 1.35kg or 1 kg 350g; 17½ metres or 17.5m or 17m and 50 cm; 2¼ hours or 2 hours 15 minutes

P38 **What's my shape?** Quadrilateral; right-angled triangle; cone; hemisphere (or cone or half ellipsoid); (square-based) pyramid; pentagon

P39 **Where does it fit?**

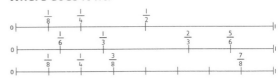

P40 **Fraction measure** $^1/_2$; $^6/_{10}$ or $^3/_5$; $^9/_{10}$; $^1/_4$; $^2/_3$; $^2/_{10}$ or $^1/_5$

Block C

P43 **10 centimetres** Answers will vary

P44 **Number sort** Answers will vary. Possible sortings include: odd numbers and not odd numbers; even numbers and not even numbers; numbers less than 10, not less than 10; numbers in the 3-times table and not in the 3-times table

Homework answers

P45 **Measuring up** 1 true; 2 false; 3 false; 4 false; 5 true; 6 true; 7 false; 8 false; 9 true; 10 true; 11 false

P46 **Bird spotting** 1 11; 2 28; 3 Thursday; 4 53; 5 answers will vary

P47 **How heavy?** 550g; 1.5kg; 3kg

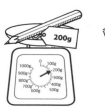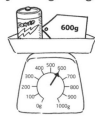

P48 **Venn diagram sort** *Is a multiple of 5:* 20, 25, 30, 35, 40, 45, 50; all remaining numbers are not a multiple of 5. *Is a multiple of 3:* 21, 24, 27, 30, 33, 36, 39, 42, 45, 48; all remaining numbers are not a multiple of 3

P49 **Bar charts** 1 8; 2 red; 3 33; 4 purple; 5 answers will vary

P50 **A day at the office** Clocks should display the following times: 8.40, 10.10, 1.50, 4.30, 5.50, 9.40

P51 **Measuring bonanza** litres; millilitres; litres; millilitres. Answers to the second part will vary

P52 **How much?** 50ml; 450ml; 600ml or $^6/_{10}$ litre or 0.6 litre; 1 litre 400ml or 1.4 litre; 15ml; 900ml or $^9/_{10}$ litre or 0.9 litre

P53 **Jugs of milk** 300ml; 650ml; 950ml; 2.5 litres; 4 litres

P54 **Which video game?** 1 puzzle games; 2 sports games; 3 33 children

Video game	Number of children
platform	🕹️ 🕹️ 🕹️
racing	🕹️ 🕹️ 🕹️ 🕹️ 🕹️
puzzle	🕹️ 🕹️
sports	🕹️ 🕹️ 🕹️ 🕹️ 🕹️ 🕹️ 🕹️ 🕹️

Block D

P57 **Telling the time** 6.10; 5.25; 9.15; 7.20; 8.50; 3.35; 4.55; 12.00; 10.40; 2.45. Answers to the second part will vary

P58 **Holiday map** Check the coordinates given against the grid

P59 **What's the time?**

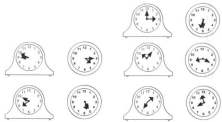

P60 **Number patterns** 16 + 8 = 24, 16 + 18 = 34, 16 + 28 = 44, 16 + 38 = 54, 16 + 48 = 64, 16 + 58 = 74, 16 + 68 = 84, 16 + 78 = 94, 16 + 88 = 104
97 − 7 = 90, 97 − 17 = 80, 97 − 27 = 70, 97 − 37 = 60, 97 − 47 = 50, 97 − 57 = 40, 97 − 67 = 30, 97 − 77 = 20, 97 − 87 = 10
24 + 7 = 31, 24 + 17 = 41, 24 + 27 = 51, 24 + 37 = 61, 24 + 47 = 71, 24 + 57 = 81, 24 + 67 = 91, 24 + 77 = 101, 24 + 87 = 111
93 − 7 = 86, 93 − 17 = 76, 93 + 27 = 66, 93 − 37 = 56, 93 − 47 = 46, 93 − 57 = 36, 93 − 67 = 26, 93 − 77 = 16, 93 − 87 = 6

P61 **Find it!** Answers will vary

P62 **What's the problem?** 51; 8 r2; 4; 9. Answers to the second part will vary

P63 **Money totals** Answers will vary

P64 **Mirror, mirror**

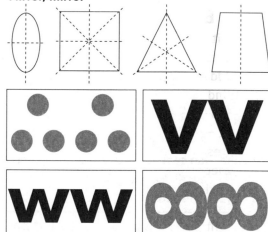

P65 **Remainder search** 1 12; 2 8; 3 6; 4 4 r4; 5 2 r4

P66 **TV times** 1 7.15pm; 2 8.20pm; 3 9.35pm; 4 11.50pm

P67 **Think of a number** 1 7; 2 16; 3 5; 4 30

P68 **Fill the jugs** 220ml; 340ml; 150ml; 410ml

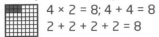

Block E

P71 Multiplication arrays

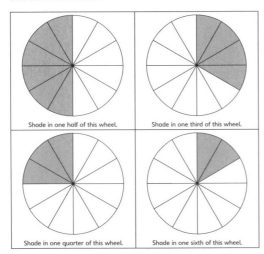

$4 \times 2 = 8$; $4 + 4 = 8$
$2 + 2 + 2 + 2 = 8$

$5 \times 4 = 20$; $5 + 5 + 5 + 5 = 20$
$4 + 4 + 4 + 4 + 4 = 20$

$6 \times 3 = 18$; $6 + 6 + 6 = 18$
$3 + 3 + 3 + 3 + 3 + 3 = 18$

$7 \times 3 = 21$; $7 + 7 + 7 = 21$
$3 + 3 + 3 + 3 + 3 + 3 + 3 = 21$

P72 Division hops **1** 8; **2** 6; **3** 7; **4** 6; **5** 8; **6** 3

P73 Wally the window cleaner 11, 17; 10, 16; 9, 15; 11, 19; 14, 19; 14, 8; 16, 12; 12, 8; 15, 5; 18, 17

P74 Make 100 50; 30; 20; 20; 40; 40; 40; 65; 23; 28

P75 Money problems 40p; 6 coins; 7p; 75p; 9p; £1; £1.50; 40p

P76 Wheel fractions

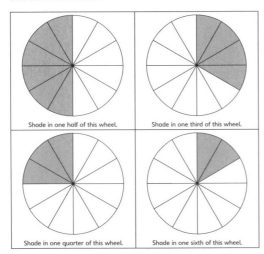

1 $^3/_6$; **2** $^2/_6$; **3** $^2/_4$

P77 Fraction search Cake $^1/_2$; pizza $^1/_3$; chocolate $^1/_{10}$; paper $^1/_4$; apples $^1/_8$

P78 Fraction shade

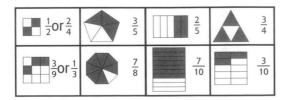

P79 Double and halve *Part 1:* 30, 15; 28, 14; 18, 9; 36, 18; 32, 16. *Part 2:* 24, 12; 26, 13; 34, 17; 38, 19. Answers to the third part will vary

P80 Multiplication and division
$5 \times 4 = 20$, $4 \times 5 = 20$, $20 \div 5 = 4$, $20 \div 4 = 5$;
$6 \times 3 = 18$, $3 \times 6 = 18$, $18 \div 3 = 6$, $18 \div 6 = 3$;
$8 \times 3 = 24$, $3 \times 8 = 24$, $24 \div 3 = 8$, $24 \div 8 = 3$;
$6 \times 5 = 30$, $5 \times 6 = 30$, $30 \div 5 = 6$, $30 \div 6 = 5$;
$9 \times 10 = 90$, $10 \times 9 = 90$, $90 \div 9 = 10$, $90 \div 10 = 9$

P81 Multiples of 2, 5 and 10
1 4, 18, 36, 88, 102, 654, 748
2 5, 25, 65, 80, 315, 450, 900
3 20, 80, 100, 120, 870
4 0, 2, 4, 6, 8
5 0, 5
6 Has 0 as its unit digit
7 Any number with 0 as its unit digit

P82 Multiplying and dividing by 10 and 100
30; 700; 250; 500; 6; 5; 80; 9; 4; 800

P83 Number square challenge Answers will vary

P84 How many? 62 pieces of fruit; 63 minutes; 18 apples

P85 Tens and units multiplication 86; 46; 72; 96; 42; 104

P86 Column addition 333; 623; 377

P87 Make a number **1** 963; **2** 369; **3** 752; **4** 257; **5** 976; **6** 235

P88 Out to lunch **1** £15; **2** £10; **3** £5; **4** £5

Puzzles and problems answers

1 **What's in the box?** 54
2 **Election selection** Bella, Neal, Penny, Ray, Stan
3 **Busker Gus** £4.70
4 **MC Squared** £1.71
5 **Time flies** 8.00pm
6 **Savour the flavours** 23
7 **Circle skills**

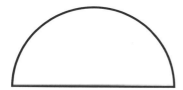

8 **Who am I?** 17 or 71
9 **Rope trick** 60cm
10 **How many wheels?** 36; 45 including steering wheels
11 **Let's operate** 42 divided by 7
12 **Mirror, mirror...** Check that the reflection of the face has been correctly drawn
13 **Who ate the pie?** A quarter
14 **Who's wrong?** Top and bottom children in the illustration are incorrect
15 **Right-angle hunt** 20
16 **Fishy fun!** 12cm, 16cm and 25cm
17 **Puzzle rings**

18 **Sunshine Sue** Wales 12 degrees, Turkey 35 degrees, France 28 degrees, Canada -7 degrees; Turkey
19 **Dozy Dizzy!** 45 minutes or ¾ hour
20 **My slug's bigger!** 12cm; check drawing is correct length
21 **Sally's tally chart**

Transport	Number of children	Frequency
Scooter	7	⊞ II
Walk	8	⊞ III
Bike	4	IIII
Car	6	⊞ I

22 **Go digital!** 35 minutes
23 **Bouncing baby** 3kg
24 **Weigh it up** 50g
25 **Letter change** b
26 **Christmas shopping** £11.91
27 **Orange juice** 700ml
28 **What comes next?** 20; 29
29 **What's my number?** 30
30 **Who's the heaviest?** Beth is heavier by 3kg (Tom is 24kg, Beth is 27kg)
31 **In the sale** £40
32 **What's in the tank?** The tank is approximately one third full; no
33 **Wolf pack** 9 wolves
34 **Same as?** 429
35 **Witch's teeth** Check that seven of the teeth have been shaded
36 **Football stickers** Wayne 20; Theo 10

SCHOLASTIC

Also available in this series:

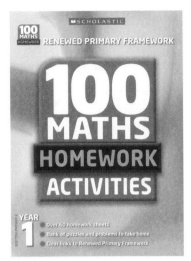

ISBN 978-1407-10216-0

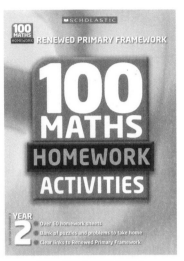

ISBN 978-1407-10217-7

ISBN 978-1407-10218-4

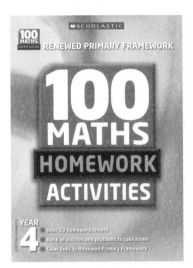

ISBN 978-1407-10219-1

ISBN 978-1407-10220-7

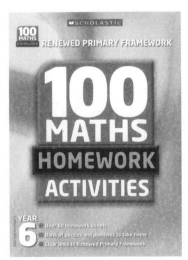

ISBN 978-1407-10221-4

To find out more, call: 0845 603 9091
or visit our website www.scholastic.co.uk